Secrets of Stage Mindreading

Ormond McGill

Crown House Publishing Limited
www.crownhouse.co.uk

First published by

Crown House Publishing Ltd
Crown Buildings, Bancyfelin, Carmarthen, Wales, SA33 5ND, UK
www.crownhouse.co.uk

and

Crown House Publishing Company LLC
4 Berkeley Street, 1st Floor, Norwalk, CT 06850, USA
www.CHPUS.com

First published 2003; reprinted 2004

British Library of Cataloguing-in-Publication Data
A catalogue entry for this book is available
from the British Library.

**International Standard Book Number
1904424015**

**Library of Congress Control Number
2003102133**

Printed and bound in the UK by
*Antony Rowe Ltd
Chippenham*

About the Author

ORMOND McGILL is known as The Dean of American Hypnotists. He is a magician and hypnotist of international reputation, and has toured many parts of the world with his exciting stage shows: East Indian Miracles, The Seance of Wonders, Real Mental Magic, South Sea Island Magic, The Concert of Hypnotism are some of their titles.

Both an authority and a performer, he brings to his writing on the subject of Genuine Stage Show Mindreading a wealth of professional knowledge. Ormond McGill is also a naturalist of prominence, his contributions in entomology and conchology being well known in those fields.

Among his previously published books are *Psychic Magic, Real Mental Magic, Science Magic, Atomic Magic, How To Produce Miracles, Entertaining With Magic* and *The New Encyclopedia of Stage Hypnotism*.

Contents

Foreword

It's Entertainment!

*"Mindreading is the popular showbiz term for
telepathic demonstrations."*

What you learn in this performance book will advance your
perception and sharpen your senses. This moment it's entertainment.
The future may find it a form of daily communication.

Ormond McGill's masterful textbook, *The New Encyclopedia of Stage
Hypnotism* has become known as 'The Bible' of stage hypnotists. It is
an international best seller. This textbook, *Secrets of Stage Mindreading*,
is a companion volume.

Being encyclopedic in scope, this book provides an authentic
background to telepathy demonstrations with scientific prestige.

In performing mindreading, you present a full-stage production.
In fact, it's a full auditorium production as many of the feats are
performed in the auditorium, right in the midst of the audience.
The show is a very personal entertainment of audience participation
that blends in perfectly with your stage hypnotism demonstrations.
Stage hypnotism and mindreading go together like ice cream and
apple pie.

It's thought-provoking entertainment that can never be forgotten.
It's the Magic of the Mind.

Charles Mignosa, C.H.T.

San Jose, CA. U.S.A.

2003

Preface

"Encyclopedic Coverage of Telepathy + Telepathic Theory + Historical Cases + Oriental Psychic Influencing + Showmanship + Self-Hypnosis For Mindreading = SECRETS OF STAGE MINDREADING"

The dictionary describes an encyclopedia as a work treating the various branches of learning.

Encyclopedias, in general, are of two types:

- type one is a comprehensive covering of many subjects.
- type two is a comprehensive covering of a specific subject.

This book on telepathy (genuine mindreading) is type two.

The dictionary describes telepathy as the communication from mind to mind by extrasensory means. It is popularly termed extrasensory perception (ESP). In a nutshell, the foregoing definition describes the phenomenon of telepathy as being the transmission of thoughts; as communication between people beyond conventional ways of using the five senses (seeing, hearing, tasting, smelling, feeling). Telepathy is the sixth sense. In such regard it belongs to the realm of the mysterious. It belongs to the realm of mind.

What does science say about telepathy? It is mysterious, yet occurs sufficiently frequently as to be worthy of serious investigation. One of the greatest scientists, Albert Einstein says about the mysterious:

> *"The most beautiful and profound thing we can experience is the mysterious. It is the source of all true art and science."*

Another great scientist – Charles Steinmetz – says about the realm of mind:

> *"In my opinion, man's next greatest discoveries will be found in his inner space, the realm of mind."*

Perhaps the easiest way to comprehend telepathy is to look upon it as a sort of 'mental radio' – in which electrical impulses leaping between neurons within the brain cause *waves of thought* to be transmitted through space from one brain to another. Upton Sinclair wrote an entire book under the title of *Mental Radio* – in which he told in detail of successful telepathic experiments conducted between himself and his wife.

Introduction

Telepathy is sufficiently mysterious as to become popular with magicians as Mental Magic (which Theo Annemann called the most adult form of magic) in which pseudo-demonstrations of telepathy are presented. You will find no pseudo-demonstrations of telepathy in this book. Its direction is exclusively *genuine telepathy*.

However, if you are looking for mental magic tricks, get a copy of any one of these three books:

- *Practical Mental Effects* by T. Annemann
- *13 Steps to Mentalism* by T. Corinda
- *The Handbook of Mental Magic* by M. Kaye

Most magic shops can supply these, and they will give you plenty of clever tricky stuff that is entertaining. But don't look for such tricky stuff in *Secrets of Stage Mindreading*. In this book, you will learn the *genuine*, and you can't beat the genuine, because mind makes the most wonderful magic of all.

Do you believe in *genuine telepathy*? In our current technological age, the majority of people do. How can it be otherwise when unexpected flashes of mental communication are constantly occurring in our daily life?

Who has not had the experience of receiving an unexpected phone call, and a thought flashes in as to whom is calling, even if you have not heard from that person for years?

Who has not found themselves thinking of an old friend almost forgotten, and on turning the corner you literally bump into the person?

Such spontaneous telepathic flashes are not infrequent. Mostly they happen between people who have a rapport with each other, such as mother and child, man and wife, sweethearts and close friends.

Rapport means a harmonious mental connection of some kind existing between the individuals involved.

Telepathy is a mental phenomenon of communication between individuals. Actually, all communication between individuals is a mental phenomenon. For our most common communication we use speech to make the connection, but it is so common we often forget that speech too, is a mental phenomenon. Telepathy is simply a mental connection made directly between people without the need for speech.

I will venture a prediction …

Speech is such an indirect way of mind-to-mind communication – so very slow. As technology advances the time will come when speech becomes more silent and telepathy makes the noise. What does the future hold?

In *Secrets of Stage Mindreading* are timeless reports of experiments in telepathy that give objective proof of its existence. Telepathy seems to be a talent, and like every talent, some people have the gift naturally whilst others have to practice to obtain it. This book will show you how to develop telepathic talent for yourself. And, if you wish, how to present a marvelous entertainment of REAL Mindreading.

Mysterious? You bet! It makes a great show!

Becoming a star with telepathy and presenting a genuine mindreading stage show will bring you great prestige, as everyone wishes they could do what you can do.

Dunninger did it……..Polgar did it…….Kreskin does it.

YOU CAN DO IT!

Part One

The Art/Science of Telepathy

Historic Résumé

Chapter One

Proof of Telepathy

Chapter One

Proof of Telepathy

It is well that you have some historic background in the research of telepathy. It provides an importance to the subject plus providing effective patter themes to embellish your show.

You stand as proof of the existence of REAL Mindreading. For example, unquestionably you will have noticed, while attending a social group, when a person makes a remark, someone across the room will exclaim, "Why that's just what I was going to say". Nearly everyone has experienced knowing what a person was going to say before the person spoke.

It is historically told that Mark Twain spoke of a plan he had frequently practiced, i.e. that of writing a letter to a person on some subject, then addressing the envelope and inserting the letter. He then tore the whole thing up instead of mailing it. Mark Twain stated that in a large percentage of such cases he would shortly receive a letter from the person to whom the destroyed letter was addressed, answering the letter that had never been sent. He tried this experiment with people sometimes many miles away. It worked for him.

Academic Evidence

Some of the best evidence for the existence of REAL Mindreading comes from university experiments in parapsychology.

The English Society for Psychic Research records the extraordinary case of the Reverend A.M. Creery and his three children. The father reported he had begun by practicing the old 'Willing Game', in which one of the party leaves the room and the company selects some object to be hidden. The person is then invited to return, while the company concentrates upon the hidden object. The person is *willed* to find the object.

In response to the group concentration, the subject would often move about the room and find the hidden object. The experiments of this nature performed by Rev. Creery and his children were remarkable. This report tells the story…

"We began by selecting the simplest objects in the room; then chose names of towns, people, dates, playing cards, and finally full lines of reading material from a book, etc. We used anything or series of ideas that those present could keep before the mind steadily. The children seldom made a mistake. As an example of their successes, seventeen playing cards were correctly named in succession. We soon found that a great deal depended upon the steadiness with which the ideas were kept before the minds of those mutually concentrating, and upon the group energy with which they *willed* the ideas to pass to the children."

The Experiments

The Society for Psychic Research began a series of careful experiments with the Creery children, which lasted for a full year. The experiments were all carefully controlled to affirm evidence for REAL Mindreading and/or Telepathy.

Having selected one of the children at random, a member of the investigating committee would take the child out of the room. While the child was completely out of sight and hearing of the experimental room, the remainder of the committee would select a card from a pack, or else write down a name or number that occurred to them at the moment. The report continues:

"On re-entering the room, the little girl would usually stand with her face to the wall. But sometimes she would stand with her eyes directed towards the floor for a period of silence varying from a few seconds to a minute. She would call out some number or card, as the case might be.

The report states that in the case of giving the names of objects chosen, the little girl scored six correctly out of fourteen. In the case of naming small objects held in the hands of members of the committee, she scored five out of six. In the case of naming cards, she scored six out of thirteen. In the case of stating names chosen by the committee she scored five out of ten."

Another of the experiments is reported as follows:

"One of the children was sent into an adjoining room, the door of which was closed. The committee, as a group, then thought of some object in the house. Absolute silence was observed. On recalling the child, she usually would appear with the mentally selected object in her hand. No one was allowed to leave the room after the object had been decided upon. The child's only instruction was to fetch one object in the house that we wanted her to bring to us. We would all concentrate upon the object chosen. In this way, we wrote down, among other things, a hairbrush – it was brought. An orange – it was brought. A wineglass – it was brought. An apple – was brought, etc."

The Society's report sums up the following results: three hundred and eighty-two trials were made in the series. In the test of naming the chosen letters on an alphabet card and numbers of two figures, the chances against the three girls were 21 to 1, 51 to 1, and 39 to 1, respectively. In the cases of the experiments of naming chosen cards it was calculated that mere *'guessing'*, according to the law of probability, would correctly name but seven and one-third out of a total of three hundred and eighty-two trials. The actual results obtained by the children were as follows:

"On the first attempt, one hundred and twenty-seven; on the second attempt, fifty-six additional, and on the third attempt, nineteen additional – making a grand total of two hundred and two successes out of a possible three hundred and eighty-two. On one occasion, five playing cards straight running were successfully named on a first trial. The mathematical chance of mere *guessing* was estimated at over a million to one."

The interest in the Creery children attracted the attention of Professor Balfour Steward, LLD, Fellow of the Royal Society. He testifies:

"In the first instance, when I was present, the thought-reader (child) was outside a door. The object being thought of was written on paper and silently handed to the company in the room. The child was called in; within a minute she told what was written on the paper, on which all were concentrating. Further, various objects in the room were thought of, and in the majority of cases the answers were correct. Also numbers were thought of and the answers were generally right. In the cases of names being thought of, some of these were in error. In the case of cards being thought of, a good many of these were right."

Subsequently the Creery children, at the home of the well-known investigator, Mr. F. W. H. Myers, in Cambridge, England, proved equally successful. The children were Mary, age 17, Alice, age 15 and

Maud, age 13. The percentage of successes obtained at Mr. Myers' house tallied very well with those obtained elsewhere.

One remarkable result was obtained though that had not been obtained before. Mary was asked to name the suit of cards chosen one after the other, e.g. hearts, diamonds, clubs, spades were drawn, observed by the committee, and then thought of. On this occasion she scored a run of fourteen straight consecutive successes.

The chances against this success were 4,782,969 to 1.

All the experiments in mindreading were scientifically conducted by the Society, in every way guarding against deception. REAL Mindreading was sought. The Creery children were excellent subjects, but by no means exceptional. By following the instructions given in this book, you can perform with high success.

The proof of REAL mindreading is mindreading.

In this *Secrets of Stage Mindreading*, you will be taken back in time to observe fascinating experiments in telepathy researched by scientific investigators of the nineteenth century. You will take a jaunt to India to learn of the Yogi modus operandi in relation to telepathy – referred to in the East as 'psychic influence.'

Part One of this book gives you a historical background for research in telepathy.

In Part Two you are shown how to present demonstrations in telepathy for yourself. With mindreading you can present a great show to thrill your audiences.

You will first learn how to perform 'Contact Mindreading' and present demonstration after demonstration. Great show business advancing from the simplex to the complex. Finally, you will learn the art of 'Non-Contact Mindreading', which is direct perception. You will advance with greater and greater skill into the realm of telepathy.

The Appendix to this book provides a method of self-hypnosis, which you can use to advance your skills as a mindreader.

Once you master how to do what this book tells you to do, and combine it with your mastery of Stage Hypnotism, you will have at your command the greatest magic in the world, for beyond question there is no greater magic than the magic of the human mind.

Chapter Two

Telepathy in the Waking State

Chapter Two

Telepathy in the Waking State

"These reports are of early research into telepathy. Feel free to carry out research yourself."

There is nothing new about telepathy. We have recognized the phenomenon for time immemorial. Here are reports from eminent investigators of their times.

Professor Barrett

In 1876, Professor Barrett of the Royal College of Science, Dublin, in a paper read before the British Association at Glasgow, drew public attention to the importance of the study of telepathy.

Up to this time, the majority of experiments with telepathy had been conducted with hypnotized people. Professor Barrett reported success with telepathy in the waking state.

The 'Willing Game' was just coming into favor and was frequently played as a party diversion. Especially among young players, cases were reported in which actions willed had been performed between subject and the person(s) willing apparently beyond the possibility of any normal means of communication. Children seemed particularly adept at it, as with the outstanding case of the Creery children previously described. Results were sufficiently striking as to warrant research.

NOTE TO READER: Why do children seem to have more success playing The Willing Game than do adults? A supposition:

Because children play the game and follow their mental impulses, while adults try to guess what they are willed to do. Playing is subjective. Guessing is objective. Telepathy is a subjective (subconscious) phenomenon.

Some people seem especially alert to telepathic influence; others are not. It seems to be an innate ability. In conducting telepathic experiments, researchers try to obtain the most responsive subjects possible.

In 1881, Professor Sidgwick, Professor Balfour Steward, Edmund Gurney and F.W.H. Myers joined with Professor Barrett, began a long series of experiments, and further seemed to establish the occurrence of telepathy in the waking state.

Some of the experiments conducted are listed here.

Transference of Tastes

This particular form of telepathy involves the impression of different tastes being mentally transmitted from researcher to percipient. In the experiments, the percipients were fully awake and blindfolded. Containers with the various substances were placed beyond their range of vision, either at a distance or outside the room. The researcher and percipient were seated on opposite sides of the room. Strict silence was observed. The researcher would take up a bit of the different substances, one at a time, and taste it while thinking what it was. Here is a report of the experiment results:

Substance tasted by the researcher was vinegar. The percipient's response was, "It has a bitter and nasty taste".

Substance tasted by the researcher was mustard. The percipient's response was, "Mustard".

Substance tasted by the researcher was a pinch of alum placed in his mouth. The percipient's response was, "Makes my lips feel puckery".

Substance tasted by the researcher was a sip of port wine. The percipient's response was, "Hard to say, something between eau de Cologne and beer".

Substance tasted by the researcher was a cube of sugar dissolving in his mouth. The percipient's response was, "Tastes sweet".

The researcher placed a pinch of salt in his mouth. The percipient's response was, "Definitely salt".

NOTE TO READER: Telepathic transference of taste sensations is highly experiential. You can experiment for yourself.

Transference of Pain

Experiments in the telepathic transference of pains are significant. Mr. Guthrie at Liverpool conducted numerous such experiments. Some trials of this kind were carried out with the same percipient, Miss R. during a nine-month period in 1884–85. The percipient on each occasion was blindfolded and seated with her back towards the rest of the party, who simultaneously pinched, pricked or scratched themselves causing a mutual pain response in the group.

Examples of this form of telepathy are given here.

	Researchers in union	**Subject response**
1.	Back of left hand pricked.	Rightly localized.
2.	Lobe of left ear pricked.	Rightly located.
3.	Left wrist pricked.	"Is it in the left wrist?" pointing to back of hand near little finger.
4.	Third finger of left hand tightly bound with wire.	Lower joint of that finger was guessed.
5.	Left wrist scratched with pins.	"It is in the left wrist like being scratched."
6.	Left ankle pricked.	Rightly localized.
7.	Spot behind left ear pricked.	No results.
8.	Right shoulder pricked.	Rightly localized.
9.	Right shoulder pricked.	Rightly localized.
10.	Hands held over open flame.	"Like a pulling pain … then tingling, like cold and hot alternately." Localized by gesture only.
11.	End tongue bitten.	"Is it the lip or the tongue?"
12.	Palm of left hand pricked.	"It is a tingling pain in the left hand here." Placing her finger on palm.
13.	Back of neck pricked.	"Is it a pricking of the neck?"

	Researchers in union	Subject response (cont)
14.	Front of left arm above elbow pricked.	Rightly localized.
15.	Spot just above left ankle pricked.	Rightly localized.
16.	Spot just above right wrist pricked.	"I am not sure, but feel a pain in my right arm just above the wrist."
17.	Inside of left ankle pricked.	Outside of left ankle guessed.
18.	Spot beneath right collar-bone pricked.	The corresponding spot on left side guessed.
19.	Back hair pulled.	No result.
20.	Inside of right wrist pricked.	Right foot guessed.

Telepathic transference of pain sensations is phenomenal. You can experiment for yourself.

NOTE TO READER: If a pain can be telepathically transferred from one person to another, it appears possible that the process could be reversed, and pain be removed by telepathic influence. Such supposition could well be of importance to hypnotherapy.

Experiments in Visual Telepathy conducted by Professsor Sir Oliver Lodge

Experiments in visual telepathy in the waking state with a percipient, Miss L., were conducted on two evenings in 1889. As reported by Professor Lodge, they would seem to leave little room for doubt that the impressions received by the percipient were of a visual nature. The transmitter on the first evening was Mr. James Birchall, who held the hand of the woman during the tests. The other person present was Professor Lodge.

Precautions were used to ensure accuracy. The object was placed behind a wooden screen between the percipient and the transmitter; at other times the percipient's eyes were bandaged and the object was held behind her. It is believed that the precautions taken were, in all cases, adequate to conceal the object from the percipient, even if her eyes had been uncovered.

In this account, any remarks given by the transmitter or Professor Lodge are entered between brackets.

Object: A blue square of silk. (Now, it's going to be color; ready.) "Is it green?" (No.) It is something between green and blue. (What shape?) Percipient drew a rhombus.

NOTE TO READER: It is not intended that this example be regarded as a success by any means. It is to be understood that so much help was given only to make a start on the first experiment, as in the example, "It's a color". When the subject is simply told, "it's an object" it is much the same as when nothing is said at all, the field of guessing is practically eliminated. The only remark made being, "Now we are ready".

Next object: A key on a black background. Percipient said, "It's an object". In a few seconds percipient said, "It's bright. It looks like a key". (Told to draw it) Percipient drew a mirror image of the key.

Next object: Three gold studs in a morocco case. Percipient said, "It is yellow … something gold … something round. There is more than one round. Yes, there seems to be more than one round. There are three rounds."

NOTE TO READER: When told to unblindfold herself and draw, percipient drew the three rounds in a row quite correctly, and then sketched around them absently the outline of the case, which seemed therefore to have been apparent to the subject though not consciously attended to. It was an interesting and striking experiment.

Next object: A pair of scissors standing partly open with their points down. Percipient said, "It is a bright object … something longways (indicating verticality). It is a pair of scissors standing up. … a little bit open." She then drew her impression, and it was correct in every particular. The object in this experiment was on a settee behind her. Its position had to be pointed out to her when, after the experience, she wanted to see the scissors.

Further Experiments in the Telepathic Transference of Visual Images by Dr. Blair Thaw

Dr. Thaw of New York used himself as percipient in the experiments. This series of tests using objects was performed on the 28th of April 1892. Professor Lodge, Edmund Gurney, and Professor Herdman of Oxford cooperated in placing the objects and concentrating on their visual images. Dr. Thaw had his eyes blindfolded and his ears stuffed with cotton. The tests proceeded:

First object: Silk pincushion in form of orange-red apple, quite round. When asked what object came to mind, Dr. Thaw said "A disc". When asked what color, he said "Red or orange". When asked what the object was, He said "Pincushion".

Second object: A short lead pencil, nearly covered by a nickel cover. The object was never seen in advance by Dr. Thaw. When asked what came into his mind, he said, "I thought of Mr. Wyatt's silver pencil".

Third object: A dark violet flower in Mr. Wyatt's buttonhole, but not known to be in the house by percipient. Percipient: "I see something dark. Not very big. Longish. Narrow. Soft. It can't be a cigarette as it is not that color." Asked about smell, said, "Not strong, but what you might call pungent; a clean smell".

The percipient had not noticed the smell before, although he was sitting by Mr. Wyatt for some time. But when afterwards he was told of the violet he said, "Yes, that was the odor he experienced".

The experiments in telepathy with Dr. Thaw concluded by seeing if he could name a couple of playing cards, and for a final test he tried to find an object in another room.

The first card looked at was the king of spades. The percipient said, "It is a spade. I sense a confusion of colors, but I can't tell what card it is."

The second card looked at was the four of clubs. After a pause the percipient said, "It is a club. This is a number card. I would say the number is four. My impression is that it is the four of clubs."

Dr. Thaw requested the objects used in each test be changed, as such seemed to help him get a clearer impression.

For a final experiment, the percipient was imagined going into the next room, and finding an object. The object was a silver inkstand.

Before he even moved from where he was, Dr. Thaw said, "I think of something bright and shiny like a silver inkstand".

We tried the experiment again and decided on another object in the next room for him to locate. A glass candlestick.

The percipient had the handkerchief taken off his eyes to be able to walk into the next room, but we did not follow him. Five minutes later we went into the room, and found him standing over the candlestick.

Dr. Thaw proved himself a really excellent telepathic percipient. He made these comments about his experience:

> "I cannot describe my sensation as an actual visualization; seemed rather to be some wholly subjective process that I knew what was being looked at. It is not, however, an easy task to analyze one's own sensations; and on the whole very probably there was visualization, but of a very faint and ideal kind."

Telepathic Experiments conducted under the direction of Mr. Malcom Guthrie

Reference has been made to the long series of telepathic experiments carried on during the years 1883–85 by Mr. Malcom Guthrie of Liverpool. During a great part of the series he was assisted by Mr. James Birchall, Honorary Secretary of the Liverpool Literary and Philosophical Society. Professor Oliver Lodge and others cooperated from time to time. Throughout there were two percipients only, Miss R. and Miss L. The experiments were conducted and the results recorded with great care and thoroughness; and the whole series, in its length, its variety, and its completeness forms perhaps the most important single contribution thus far recorded of experimental telepathy in the waking state. In July 1885 summing up the results attained, Mr. Guthrie writes:

> "We have now a record of 535 experiments, and I recently set myself the task of classifying them into the four classes of successful, partially successful, misdescriptions, and failures.

The following is a summary of the work done, classified to the best of my judgement.

All visual using letters, figures, cards, numbers and names, including 94 tests with taste and smells, and 52 with transference of pain sensations. Some of the tests were performed with contact (gripping hand of the percipient) and some with no contact. Contact seemed to increase successful results. Results stand at 237 successful, 82 partially successful, 68 misdescriptions, 70 failures." (*A complete record of this report in telepathy in the waking state is retained in the Guthrie files.*)

Thus far, these reports of research into the phenomena of telepathy have all been about outstanding men during the latter half of the 19th century.

Continuing Research with Dr. Joseph Rhine

The research into telepathy conducted by Dr. Joseph Rhine, at Duke University, has taken the experimental effort on into the 20th century. Using a consistent testing of percipients with the Zener Card symbols of square, cross, triangle, star and wavy lines it has been possible to get statistical records of results obtained using university students as percipient volunteers.

Dr. Rhine has been instrumental in establishing a Department of Parapsychology at Duke University.

In the course of experimenting with telepathy, various techniques have come along that seem to aid the process. Most important is that both the agent and the percipient should be relaxed during the experiments. A rule-of-thumb for both to hold is '*Less and less try to make things happen and more and more just let things happen*'. In other words, in performing tests in thought transference make the effort without effort.

Thought transference should be a gentle flowing, not a struggle of desperate concentration. In the telepathing of the image of an object for example, the agent just relaxes and keeps looking at the object, and forms an image of the object in his or her mind, while the percipient just relaxes and allows the vision of the image to come in of its own accord.

Emulating children when you perform telepathy often is effective. Children are often far better at telepathy than adults because they believe they can rather than they can't. Children frequently report all manner of telepathic experiences until adults tell them to stop fantasizing.

It has been found that working in close unity between agent and percipient develops successful results. For developing rapport between agent and percipient try this:

> The next time you experiment with telepathy, you and percipient take three deep breaths together, and see how much it helps.

> I have often used this process in performing telepathy with a person.

> Both stand erect, facing each other. Hands hang at your sides, but are held out about six inches from body. Close your eyes and together take three deep breaths, slowly in unison.

> After exhaling the last breath, repeat out loud, "We are bringing Cosmic Energy into ourselves to mutually enhance our telepathic communication." Pause and wait.

> Let the energy flow into your hands. Both you and the subject will note a tingling of energy like a mild electric current coming into the fingers. Perform this process three times. Each time the flow of incoming energy will seem to increase. This incoming energy flow has been called 'The Force'.

Often using this process in advance of experimenting with telepathy seems to increase successful results.

Also, working with the percipient while in hypnosis frequently produces striking telepathic phenomena, as described in the next Chapter.

Chapter Three

Telepathy in the Hypnotic State

Chapter Three

Telepathy in the Hypnotic State

As has been mentioned, the majority of experimenting with telepathy has been with people while hypnotized. Somehow hypnosis offers peculiar facilities for the transmission of thought and sensations. Why?

It is possible that the superior telepathic sensitiveness of people in hypnosis is in some measure due to freedom from the business of daily activities. Hypnosis affords an opportunity to explore, and functions in, the deeper abysses of the mind undisturbed. Also, there are indications that the hypnotic state develops a specialized manifestation of rapport, which exists between the transmitter ('agent') and the receiver ('percipient') in the performance of telepathy.

The close association of the telepathic activities with the subconscious, which emerges in hypnosis, very likely will throw light on the evolution of the faculty itself. However that may be, and no matter how remarkable telepathic experiences may occur in the waking state, there can be no question that the most remarkable results in experimental telepathy so far recorded are those experienced by people in hypnosis. The early hypnotists, producing hypnosis by mesmeric procedure, often reported subjects performing actions by telepathic commands without need of verbal direction.

Telepathic Transmission of Taste and Pain

This type of thought transmission has been previously discussed with examples given. The telepathic transmission of taste and pain sensations seems to become ever more pronounced when performed in the hypnotic state. In such regard, Dr. Dufay quotes the following from a letter received by him in February 1889 from Dr. Azam, the celebrated hypnotist/physician:

> "I believe along with many other medical men that a telepathic transference of sensations occurs in the hypnotic state. I will

quote two cases in which I think I took all necessary precautions before being convinced of their truth.

About 1853 or 1854, I had under my care a young woman with confirmed hysteria: nothing was easier than to put her to sleep (hypnosis) by various means. I consider myself entitled to state that while holding her hand my unspoken thoughts were transferred to her, but upon this I do not insist, error being possible.

But the transmission of a definite sensation seemed to me to be absolutely certain. This is how I proceeded:

Having put the patient to sleep, and seated myself by her side, I leaned towards her and dropped my handkerchief behind her chair; then, while stooping to pick it up, I quickly put into my mouth a pinch of common salt, which, unknown to her, I had beforehand put into the pocket of my waistcoat. The salt being absolutely without smell, it was impossible that the patient should have known that I had some in my mouth; but as soon as I raised myself again I saw her face express disgust, and she moved her lips about. "That is very nasty," she said, "Why did you put salt in my mouth?"

In my opinion, the use of hypnosis very much amplifies the reception of direct thought transference. To many investigators the more salient phenomena of the trance – hallucination, anesthesia, catalepsy, etc. have distracted attention from what may ultimately prove to be the most fruitful line of inquiry."

Telepathy Experiments reported by Dr. Liebeault

The following record of experiments of telepathy in hypnosis, from Dr. Liebeault of Nancy, was presented in 1886.

The first series of experiments with telepathy in hypnosis were made on the afternoon of the 10th December 1885, in Dr. Liebeault's house at Nancy. There were present, in addition, Madame S., Dr. Brullard, and Professor Liegeois, who acted as agents (telepathic transmitters), and Mademoiselle M, the percipient in the tests.

The percipient was hypnotized by Professor Liegeois and experiments were made with diagrams. In two cases the design of a water-bottle (carafe) and a table with a drawer and drawer-knob were exactly reproduced. Precautions had, of course, been taken to conceal the original designs from the percipient.

In another experiment, Professor Liegeois wrote the word MARRIAGE. Mdlle M., while in profound hypnosis, then wrote "Monsieur". Then she said "Decanter … no pitcher … no. (What is the letter?) It is an L … no, it is an M". Then, after thinking for some minutes, "There is an *i* in the word, and also an *e*. There are six letters in the word … no seven". When she had found all the letters and their places, she could still not find the letter *r*. After a few minutes it was suggested to her that she should try combinations with the different consonants, and finally she wrote MARRIAGE.

Further experiments were made by Dr. Liebeault, in conjunction with M. Stanislas de Guaita, on the 9th of January 1886. The percipient, in this case was Mademoiselle Louise L., who was hypnotized by Dr. Liebeault. The telepathic experiments reported here are very interesting. The third in the series and the two subsequent trials with Mdlle Camille Simon present illustrations of telepathic hallucination superimposed upon a basis of reality.

Dr. Liebeault, in order that no hint should be given even in a whisper, wrote on a piece of paper, "Mademoiselle, on waking, will see her black hat transformed into a red one". The paper was then passed around to all witnesses. Then Liebeault and De Guaita placed their hands silently on the hypnotized woman's forehead, mentally formulating the sentence agreed upon.

After being told she would see something unusual in the room, the young woman was awakened. Without a moment's hesitation she fixed her eyes upon the hat, and with a burst of laughter exclaimed that it was not her hat; she would have none of it. It was the same shape certainly, but this farce had gone far enough – we had to give her back her own. We asked, "Come now, what difference do you see?" She answered, "You know quite well. You have eyes like me". We had to press her for some time before she would say what change had come over her hat; surely we were making fun of her. At last she said, "Surely you can see for yourselves that it is red".

We were forced to put an end to her hallucination by telling her that her hat would presently resume its usual color. The doctor breathed on it, and when it became, in her eyes, her own again, she consented to take it back. Directly afterwards she remembered nothing of her hallucination.

Signed,   A.A. Liebeault
Stanislas De Guita
Nancy
9th January 1886

Dr. Liebeault tells of another very successful experience with telepathy in hypnosis:

"We had one very successful experiment with a young girl of about fifteen, Mdlle. Camille Simon, in the presence of M. Brullard and several other people. I gave her a telepathic suggestion that on waking from hypnosis she should see her hat, which was brown, changed to yellow. I then put her *enrapport* with all the others, and I passed around a slip of paper indicating my suggestion, and asking them to think of the same thing. But by a lapse of memory not unusual for me, I did not think of the particular color I had written down. I had a distinct impression that she would see her hat *red*. On awaking her, I told her she would see something representing our common thought. When she awakened she wondered at the color of her hat. 'It is brown', she said. After having thought for a while, she assured us that really it did not look at all the same, that she could not quite define the color, but that it seemed to her a sort of *yellow-red*. Then I remembered my aberration. In the present case the others thought of yellow; I of red; thus the object appeared yellow and red to the awakened somnambulist, which indicates that mental suggestion may very well be an echoing of the thoughts of many minds."

Dr. Liebeault on 3rd June 1886 tells of an interesting example of temporary latency of the telepathic impression. He writes:

"In another experiment with the same young girl, it was suggested mentally to her, by several people, that on waking from being hypnotized she would see a black cock walking in the room. For a considerable time after waking, nearly half-an-hour, she said nothing, although I told her she would see something.

It was another half-an-hour after that, having gone into the garden and looked by chance into my little courtyard she came running back to us to say, 'Ah, I know what I was to see: it was a black cock. This came into my head when I was looking at your cock'. My cock is greenish-black on the wings, tail and breast; everywhere else he is yellowish-white. Here we have an idea caused by the sight of a real object associated with a fictitious idea mentally transmitted by the people present."

Further Experiments with Telepathy in Hypnosis

Between the beginning of July and the end of October 1889, a series of tests in hypnotic telepathy, using numbers, were conducted by Mrs. Sidgwick, with the assistance of Mr. C.A. Smith and Professor Sidgewick. In the tests small, wooden Loto counters that had numbers from 10 to 90 printed on them were used. There were 81 counters placed in a bag, and thoroughly mixed.

At random, Mr. C.A. Smith drew a counter from the bag and placed it in a little wooden box – it was effectively concealed from the view of the percipient. The percipient, who had been previously placed in the hypnotic state by Mr. Smith, sat with eyes closed and was ready to receive impressions of the number drawn. No remarks were made during the experiments, and the results were recorded by Mrs. Sidgwick.

Mr. Smith proved to be the best telepathic transmitter of the group but he failed to produce any results when the percipient was not hypnotized.

The percipient was Mr. P., a clerk in a wholesale business, aged about nineteen, who had been frequently hypnotized by Mr. Smith. He went into a hypnotic trance quickly. As he went into trance his eyes turned upwards, before his eyelids closed.

Here is a table of the experiments in telepathy with Mr. P. while in hypnosis:

S. = Smith (transmitter of numbers as selected at random from bag, and then concealed in box).

P. = hypnotized percipient in telepathic tests using numbers.

Number drawn	*Number guessed and remarks*
87	S: "Now P. you are going to see numbers. I will look at them, and you will see them." P: (almost immediately) "I see 87. You asked me if I saw a number. I saw an 8 and a 7. I saw nothing more."
19	P: "I see number 18." S: "What are the numbers on?" P: "Appears to me like brass numbers on a door."
24	P: (after a pause) "I keep on looking. I see an 8 and a 4."
35	P: "I see a 3 and a 5. 35." S: "How did that look?" P: "I saw first a 3 and then a 5, then 35."
28	P: "I see 88. One number is behind the others, then one popped forward, and I see two eights." (Illustrated it with his fingers.)
20	P: "I can't see anything yet." S: "You will directly." P: "23." S: "You saw that clearly." P: "Not so plain as the other." S: "Which did you see best?" P: "The 2."
27	P: "I can see 7, and I think a 3 in front of it. Yes, I see a 7." S: "Make sure of the first number." P: "The 7 is gone now. The 3 changed to a 2."
48	S: "Here's another one, P." This remark, though not always recorded, almost always began each experiment until July 27th, when, to avoid the possibility of unconscious indications, Mr. Smith adopted the plan of not speaking at all. P: "Another two, you mean. You say another one, but there are always two." S: "Yes, two." P: "There's only one, an 8." Some remarks here are not recorded. We think that Mr. Smith said there were two, and told him to look again.

Number drawn	*Number guessed and remarks (cont.)*
	P said he saw 4. Mrs. Sidgwick: "Which came first?" P: "The 8 first, then the 4 to the left, so it would have been 48, I would like to know how to do that trick."
20	P: "A 2 and an 0; went away very quickly that time."
71	P: "71."
36	P: "3 ... 36."
75	P: "I might turn around. Should I see them just the same over there?" (Changed his position so as to sit sideways in the chair, and looking away from Mr. Smith.) S: "Well, you might try." P: "I don't think I see so well this way." (He did not move however.) "I see a 7 and a 5 – 75. Why don't you let them both come at once? I believe I should see them better if you let me open my eyes." (No notice was taken of this.)
17	S: "Now then, P. here's another." P: "Put it there at once." (Then, after some time) "You've only put a 4 up. I see 7." S: "What's the other number?" P: "I see 7. S: "Have a look again." P: "I see it now." S: "Which way are they arranged?" P: "I see 1 first, the 7 second."
52	S: "Here's another." P: "52. I saw that at once. I'm sure there's some game about it." (He has said something about this before, when the number was slow in coming. He said Mr. Smith was making game of him, and pretending to look when he was not looking.)
76	P: "76"

It will be observed that P. always spoke of 'seeing' the numbers, but as a matter of fact his eyes were closed, or appeared to be closed, throughout the experiments, and the pupils, as already stated, were introverted, at least at the start of the trance. That the impressions were of a visual nature there can be no reasonable doubt. This may have been due to Mrs. Sidgwick's suggestion to the percipient that he would *see* the numbers, though it seems equally probable that it was owing to the fact that Mr. Smith's impression was a visual one. That the vision in most cases was perfectly distinct seems equally clear. It is difficult to decide whether impressions received under such circumstances, with the eyes closed, are properly to be classed as hallucination. (For such impressions seen with closed eyes Kandinsky has proposed the name *pseudo-hallucinations*.)

That under appropriate conditions the percipient was capable of rising to the level of an externalized sensory hallucination, the following experiments, which took place later on the same day, 6th July, seem to show.

A blank sheet of paper was spread out on the table. P. was told that he would see numbers on it, and was then partially awakened and his eyes opened. He was told at once to look at the paper and see what came, but he saw nothing for some time. Different stages of the hypnotic trance frequently exhibit different and mutually elusive memories, and P. now had evidently forgotten all about the previous state in which he had been guessing numbers, and appeared so wide awake that it was hard to believe that he was not in a completely normal condition.

Mr. Smith stood behind him, and further experiments continued:

Number drawn	Number seen on the paper and remarks
18	P: "23." S: "Is that what you can see?" P: "Yes" (but he added later than he did not see it properly).
87	P: "A 7, 0. Oh no, 8, 78. Funny! I saw a 7 and a little 0, and then another came on top of it, and made an 8."
37	P: "There's a 4, 7." Asked where, he offered to trace it and drew 47 in figures 1½ inches long. (He had on previous occasions been asked to trace hallucinations.)
44	P: "No. I see 5, 4; it's gone again." S: "All right look at it." P: "45." S: "Sure?" P: "There is a 4; the other is not so clear. Then quickly, Two fours; 44."

Number drawn	*Number seen on the paper and remarks (cont)*
37	P: (after long gazing): "37." S: "Is that what you see P?" S: "It's gone. I am pretty sure I saw 37."

Similar trials were carried out with other percipients, Misses B., T., and W.

In all, 644 trials were made with the transmitter in the same room with the percipients, of which 131 were successful, that is both digits were given correctly, though in 14 out of the 131 cases in reverse order. The chance of success was, of course, 1 in 81, and the most probable number of complete successes was therefore 8.

218 trials were also made with Mr. Smith in a different room from the percipient but of these there were only 9 successes: 8 of these successes occurred in the course of 139 trails with P: 79 trials with T yielded only one success.

NOTE TO READER: It has been observed that the early hypnotists, using the mesmeric type of induction, often reported that their subjects responded to unspoken commands. A thought in the mind of the mesmerist caused an immediate reaction in the mind of the subject. The phenomena seemed definitely telepathic. With the advent of the psychological approach of verbal suggestion, these phenomena largely disappeared. For the benefit of contemporary research into telepathy in the hypnotic state, I include the Mesmeric Technique, which may prove of use to your personal experimental research.

The Mesmeric Method of hypnotizing

Mesmerism seeks to give mentally directed energy from the operator to the subject. The suggestions, being given silently, via *thinking* of the suggestions, flow into the subject along with the directed flow of energy. Mesmerism is definitely a telepathic process of hypnotizing.

The Modus Operandi[1]

Have the subject take a seat opposite you so that you face each other. Take their right hand in your left hand and their left hand in your

[1] *The New Encyclopedia of Stage Hypnotism, pp. 250–52. Published by Crown House Publishing Ltd., Wales, UK, 1996.*

right. Then firmly grip hands, allowing the balls of thumbs to meet.

Lean forward in your chair until your knees touch, and your face is about twelve inches from the subject's face.

Have the subject gaze steadily into your eyes as you gaze back in turn. You will experience an electric-like sensation passing between your hands. Then explain:

"You will soon feel a tingling in your hands as I grip them. This tingling sensation will gradually extend up your arms to the shoulders, and a sort of numbness will creep over your body. Do not be uneasy at any sensations which may occur, and do not allow yourself to wonder at anything which may happen. Just make yourself receptive to the telepathic influence that I will project into your mind and body. As the numbness proceeds and you find you can no longer bear to keep your eyes open and fastened upon mine, close them, and they will not come open again. You will then pass into a profound trance state, and your entire body will feel warm, and you will sense a gentle current, which will seem to you like a surge of body electricity, and the pulse in your thumbs will throb."

As you give these suggestions, THINK of them as occurring to the subject. You are using a telepathic method of hypnotizing.

Continue:

"When your eyes are closed, I will make passes over you that will fill you with bioenergy (animal magnetism). It will feel like a warmth coming into your body and you will pass deep down into mesmeric sleep."

Now rise and stand before the subject and make long sweeping passes in front of their body. This makes your own energy increase the magnetic influence and telepathic responsiveness. Distribute the force evenly throughout the body of the subject.

The Mesmeric Method employs a minimum of verbal suggestion. In fact, the less verbal suggestion used the better. Let your mind speak directly to the mind of the subject. THINK how relaxed the subject is becoming, how comfortable, and how deeply the subject is becoming entranced.

Continue your passes down over the subject's body in a slow sweeping movement, terminating at the knees. At the end of the pass, throw your hands outward and shake them. Turn your hands palms inward again, and continue the passes. Make passes down the front of the body and then makes passes on the rear of the body. Passes are made without contact – passing through the subject's aura about four inches from the body's surface.

All the time you are making the passes THINK of your regular suggestion-formulae that you use for inducing conventional hypnosis. But remember, in mesmerism, *think them rather than speak them.*

You will find mesmerism will entrance the subject while increasing their psychic energy, and that many of your mental commands can follow in a wordless manner. Using mesmerism you will find telepathic phenomena occurring – effects so noted by early hypnotists.

To arouse the subject from the mesmeric trance, reverse your body- sweeping passes – making the passes upwards rather than downwards. Make the passes upwards and throw off the energy.

Think AWAKEN. Blow on the subject's forehead and the arousal will be complete.

Of all types of telepathic experimenting, using the Mesmeric Method of hypnotizing is much to be desired.

NOTE TO READER: As a hypnotist, it is heartedly recommended that you experiment with these 19th century trials with telepathy, bringing such research up-to-date into the 21st century.

Chapter Four

Telepathic Control of Movements

Chapter Four

Telepathic Control of Movements

"A thought always produces a movement in the body, so closely that the thought and body movement can literally be conceived as ONE."

When a thought comes in as a telepathic impulse to perform a physical action of some kind it enters the realm of Telepathic Control of Movements.

It is well to consider this principle with care, as it is basic to the performance of REAL Mindreading that you will learn in PART TWO of this *Secrets of Stage Mindreading*. For this purpose, it is well that we continue to go back in time and explore outstanding research in telepathy.

In the two preceding Chapters experiments have been discussed where the impression was received by the percipient, more-or-less accurately, as a telepathic transmission from the transmitter. We will now consider cases in which the transmission of a thought is more than just a mental image. Such cases demonstrate that the telepathic impulse can lead to a physical action on the part of the percipient.

It was frequently stated by the older mesmerists that the operator, by a silent act of will, could induce a responsive subject to do, or refrain from doing, some prescribed or customary action. By following the clue thus obtained, the Committee on Mesmerism appointed by the Society of Psychic Research in 1882 succeeded in obtaining positive results on such phenomena.

Inhibition of Action by Silent Willing

The first experiments of this kind were conducted by Dr. Sidney Beard, who took an active interest in such research. Dr. Beard could be hypnotized easily, and would sit in a chair with closed eyes. Then a list of twelve 'Yes' and 'No' responses, in arbitrary order, was written by members of the investigating committee. It was then successively *willed* that the hypnotized man would respond or not respond, in accordance to the list.

A tuning fork was then struck, and held next to the hypnotized doctor's ear. One of the committee asked the question, "Do you hear?" This was done twelve times in succession, Doctor Beard answering or failing to answer on each test in accordance to the 'Yes' or 'No' of the written list – that is to say, with the silent-will of the transmitter. The results were remarkably successful.

Doctor Beard's personal account of his experiences was as follows:

> "During the experiments of 1st January, 1883, when I was mesmerized (the most popular term for hypnotism in that period of its history), I did not lose consciousness at any time, but only experienced a sensation of total numbness in my limbs. When the trial as to whether I could hear or not hear sound was made, I heard the sound distinctly each time, but somehow I felt unable to acknowledge that I heard them. I seemed to know each time what the mesmerist wished me to say, as I opened my mind to the operator at the commencement of the experiment. In other words, I seemed to respond to a telepathic command of the mesmerist while under the mesmeric influence."

Trials in Telepathic Body Responses by Professor Barrett

Further trials of the same kind were carried on in November 1883 by Professor Barrett at his house in Dublin. The hypnotist and agent was Mr. G. A. Smith; the percipient was a young man named Fernley, a stranger to the hypnotist. Fernley was placed in profound hypnosis using the mesmeric process.

In the first series of trials, Professor Barrett told the subject, "Form your hand into a fist. You will be able to open your hand or unable to open your hand in accordance to 'Yes' or 'No' written on alternate cards. Each card selected in the trial was held in sight of Mr. Smith but out of sight of the percipient. Mr. Smith, who was not in contact with the subject, directed his 'silent will' in accord to the written directions. In twenty experiments conducted under these conditions, there were only three failures.

Later, to quote Professor Barrett:

> "To avoid any possible indication as to what the subject was to do, for example being able to open his fist or unable to open his fist, in accordance to the random card selection, in all cases, I shuffled the cards face downwards, and then handled the top card that came with its unknown 'Yes' or 'No' to Mr. Smith, who looked at the card and *willed* the subject's hand response to be in accordance to the command.

> I noted down the result, and then, and not until then, looked at the card."

A final experiment was made when Mr. Smith was taken across the hall and placed in the dining room, at a distance of about thirty feet from the subject – two closed doors intervening. Under these conditions, three further successful trials were made.

At this point, the subject dropped deeper into somnambulism, and made no further responses.

Professor Barrett conducted further experiments with telepathy of this nature. Almost all the experiments were uniformly successful.

In interpreting these results, there is no justification for assuming direct control by the transmitter over the mind of the percipient. Nor do such experiments indicate that the will of the transmitter dominates the will of the subject. There is nothing to indicate that the impulses transferred directly affected the body of the subject, or even the sensory centers in anyway.

In the absence of any direct evidence, it is probable that only the higher brain centers are involved in telepathy, and the thought-transmitted idea is reflected until it assumes a form of sensory hallucination.

Upon this view no fundamental distinction needs be drawn between the results described and those now to be considered. It would seem the question is not one of transference of will or of a motor impulse. It appears that what is actually transmitted from the transmitter is probably only a simple idea. Its subsequent translation into action is as much the work of the percipient's mind as it is the work of the transmitter's mind.

With regard to the particular effects produced, it must be remembered that the prime characteristic of the hypnotic state is its openness to suggestion, and especially to suggestions coming through a particular channel. In telepathic experiments it is the establishment of this suggestible state, which consists essentially of the suppression of the controlling faculties which normally pass judgement on the suggestions received from without, and selection of those which are to find response in action, rather than the subject's surrendering of will. So when the subject responded to our questions he did what his natural courtesy led him to do; when he maintained silence his tendency to respond to the stimulus of our questions of 'Yes' or 'No' responses was momentarily overcome by the stronger stimulus of the idea received from the transmitter. But the superior efficacy of the idea so transferred resulted not from any impulsive quality of the idea itself, but from the previously established relationship between transmitter and percipient. The fact that experiments of this kind have rarely succeeded in the waking state is no doubt due to the inferior suggestibility of that state.

NOTE TO READER: Some suppositions to have fun with. The reader is invited to experiment with telepathic experiences for him or herself, and form their own opinions.

Telepathic Action originated by Silent Willing

In relation to telepathy, Dr. Blair Thaw records four experiments that present a modification of 'The Willing Game'. In most Willing Game telepathy experiments the percipient was willed to perform a certain action by a group while the percipient was in the same room with the group. In this series of four experiments, the percipient was willed to fetch an object from another room that was entirely out of sight of the transmitters.

Report by Dr. Blair Thaw of these four experiments conducted on 7th April 1892:

Mrs. Thaw, Percipient.

Mr. M.H. Wyatt and Dr. Thaw, Transmitters by willing action.

In the four experiments an object was selected in another room and the percipient was sent to find it by telepathic influence. No clue was given as to where it was in the room.

1st object selected – A wooden cupid, from a corner-piece in the room, with other objects on it. The percipient first brought a photo from the lower shelf of the corner-piece, then said, "It's the wooden cupid."

2nd object selected – A matchbox on the mantel. The percipient seemed confused at first and brought two photos, then said, "It's the brass match box on the mantel".

3rd object selected – A vellum book on a table, among twenty other books. A bag from under one window was brought out first. Then the percipient went to the table, put her hand on the book, then went to a bag and took it up, then back to the table and took the vellum book and then again the bag, and then appeared with both. The percipient was in sight of the transmitters during this time, but did not see them.

4th object selected – A book on a small table among ten others books. Missed.

In commenting on these experiments, Dr. Thaw was inclined to attribute some of the results to 'an indistinct motor impulse of some kind, leading the percipient near the object'.

Experiments of a somewhat similar nature are recorded by Dr. Ochorowicz (Le Suggestion Mentale). The subject in this case, Madame M., was placed in a deep hypnotic state, a condition in which she would usually remain motionless until aroused by the doctor. Under these circumstances, Dr. Ochorowicz conducted upwards of forty experiments in conveying mental commands, a large proportion of which were executed by the subject with more-or-less exactness.

Some experiments made by Dr. Gilbert on Madame B., and recorded by Professor Pierre Janet also met with similar success. Dr. Gilbert, however, communicated the mental commands by touching Madame B.'s forehead.

Production of Local Anesthesia by Telepathy

In concluding this Chapter on telepathic control of movements, a completely different form of body awareness telepathy is presented, without the consciousness of the percipient, but differing in the important particular that no deliberate or conscious effort on the part of the percipient could have produced such phenomena.

In experiments carried out with various subjects at intervals through the years 1883–87, Mr. Edmund Gurney seems to have shown that it was possible, by means of the expressed will of the transmitter, to produce local anesthesia in certain people. Mr. G.A. Smith assisted in the experiments.

Conducting Experiments in Local Anesthesia by Telepathy

The subject was seated at a table with his hands passed through holes in a screen, so they were completely concealed from his view. Mr. G.A. Smith then held his hand at a distance of two or three inches from the protruding fingers of the subject (as indicated by Mr. Burney) while willing that the selected finger should become rigid and insensible. On subsequently applying appropriate tests, it was found that the selected finger would actually become rigid and be insensible to pain.

Mr. Gurney and Mr. Smith performed 160 tests of this telepathic anesthesia effect:

- in 124 cases the finger that Mr. Smith's hand was over and that was being concentrated upon was affected

- in 16 cases Mr. Gurney and Mr. Smith were both successful

- in 13 cases Mr. Gurney was successful and Mr. Smith failed

- in the remaining 7 cases no effect at all was produced

It is noteworthy that in a series of 41 similar trials, in which Mr. Smith, while holding his hand over the selected subject's finger and willing that no effect should occur, the action caused no effect to be experienced.

The anesthesia effect was tested by pricking, burning or by the passing of an electrical current through the telepathically made insensible finger. In the majority of the successful trials the insensibility was shown to be proof against all assaults, however severe.

At the end of each trial, the subject was requested to open and close his hand showing returned flexibility.

In these earlier experiments it seemed essential to success that Mr. Smith's hand should be in close proximity to that of the subject without an intervening barrier. Later it was found that the screening did not affect the results. Mr. Gurney was inclined to regard this kind of telepathic influence as being, as he phrased it, "a kind of nervous induction operating on the affected part of the percipient's organism".

NOTE TO READER: In these early experiments, one is reminded of the remarkable surgical operations performed by Dr. James Esdaile in India using mesmerism as his anesthetic. It may be that telepathy of nullification of pain from the operator can nullify pain in the receptive patient. In such regard, it would seem important to recognize that the physician's mental attitude (telepathy) is important to the healing of the patient.

Chapter Five

Oriental Telepathy Techniques

Chapter Five

Oriental Telepathy Techniques

In the study and performance of genuine telepathy it is an advantage to get some knowledge of Oriental Telepathy Techniques. In this we move from the West to the East. The phenomenon of telepathy is positively accepted in eastern countries. During the wars in India, the British were amazed at how knowledge of their troop movements became known across the continent from Calcutta to Bombay. It has been claimed the Hindus used a form of thought-transference – 'mental radio'.

The Western terms of telepathy and hypnotism are not much used in the Orient. Such terms as 'chakras' 'prana', 'akasha', etc. are familiar in the East.

Chitta is the Yoga term for what forms the basis of mental influence (telepathy). It is looked upon as 'mind stuff'.

Oriental hypnosis/telepathy is regarded as a dynamic situation existing between both parties. Each visualize they are holding a bowl of chitta. The transmitter concentrates his mind upon the surface of his chitta causing ripples of thought upon its surface that resonate similar ripples of thought upon the visualized bowl of chitta the percipient holds. This is thought-transference, as it is looked upon in the East. This is far from the academic understanding of telepathy by Western science, yet actually is the same telepathic phenomenon expressed in this rather poetic form.

Common to all forms of Oriental Telepathy is the custom of the operator (in most cases one of the Yogi cast) forming a mental-picture of the thing and/or thought desired to be mentally transmitted. This produces a thought-form that must next be charged with prana. Prana is the vital energy of life. It comes into the body with the breath. It is not the breath, but it is produced most strongly by the practice of Rhythmic Breathing (Pranayama). Rhythmic Breathing is accomplished by using the following process:

Take your pulse beat and get the rhythm of your heart. Establish this rhythm in yourself so you know it instinctively, then breathe like this:

- breathe in slowly covering a period of six heart beats
- hold the breath for three heartbeats
- exhale for six heartbeats
- establish this rhythm to your breathing continually

Rhythmic Breathing greatly increases your vitality, and vitality increases your telepathy.

When you have learned how to visualize strongly and when you have learned to bring in prana to strengthen your visualization, you are well on your way to perform telepathy by Oriental methods.

Here are some further instructions.

Using the crystal ball to advance your power of visualization

First, rid your mind of all belief that there is some miraculous power inherent in the crystal ball. The crystal ball is simply an efficient instrument serving as a focal center on which to focus and concentrate your mental forces in the process of visualization. Regard the crystal ball precisely as a scientist would regard the lens of his microscope. In this practice of advancing your powers of visualization the crystal operates akin to a magnifying glass, which in focusing the rays of the sun can generate enough heat to start a fire: the crystal ball focuses the currents of your mental energy in a similar manner.

You can obtain a crystal ball from any store that handles crystals. A solid glass ball three inches in diameter is fine. Be sure the glass is free from flaws, as they are distracting.

Now, determine your purpose in using the crystal ball is for increasing your powers of visualization – the better you can visualize, the more your ability in telepathy increases. Advancing your ability in telepathy is your objective. Follow these rules:

1. Have the room in which you practice crystal visualization free from disturbing outside sights and sounds. Remove all mirrors.

   The tone of the room should be subdued, and the temperature comfortable.

   All light in the room should be low key when you practice. In other words, use moderate lighting that is neither too bright nor too dark. In placing the crystal in the room, arrange it so the rays of light do not reach it directly, nor be reflected in or from it. The light source should always be from behind your back.

2. The crystal ball may either rest on its stand or lie unsupported on the table in front of you. Or if you prefer, simply hold it in your hand. Having the crystal resting on a square of black velvet also works well.

3. In concentrating upon the crystal, relax as you gaze at it. This is called 'Crystal Gazing'. Never strain or overly tire your eyes. Make it a pleasant experience for yourself. As you gaze at the crystal do not stare at it. Do not avoid blinking your eyes. Be completely natural in your practice. Make it fun, like when you play a game.

   Sometimes an interesting technique is to make two funnels of your hands, gazing through them at the crystal, as you would through a pair of opera glasses. Do whatever you most enjoy.

4. Perform your practice in visualization with the crystal ball when you are alone. When other people are present it can be disturbing. Solitude is an aid to concentration.

5. Acquire proficiency in using the crystal gradually; make your sessions no longer than ten minutes at the start. After a while, this period may be increased to fifteen minutes. Later on, the period may be lengthened to thirty minutes, and so on. But, you should impose a final time limit of one hour. Sitting Crystal Gazing for longer than one hour is not advised.

6. Your success in using the crystal does not depend upon your ability to see pictures in the crystal, as many seek to do in Crystal Gazing. That is not your purpose in this practice; your purpose is to advance your ability to visualize strongly within your mind to advance your telepathic abilities. As you objectively gaze upon the crystal, subjectively form mental pictures within your mind – not in the crystal. The mental picture is to be seen in 'the mind's eye', as it were, and not by your physical eyes as a reflection in the crystal. The visualization is in "that which is seen by the inner eyes is that which is the bliss of solitude", as it is expressed in Yoga.

Visualization is difficult for some people and easy for others. There is a certain knack required to master the process. But proficiency will come with practice.

The oriental processes of Rhythmic Breathing to bring in prana and the Crystal Gazing to enhance your power of visualizing will be invaluable to your developing skill with telepathy and thus improve your performance of mindreading upon the stage.

Chapter Six

Silent Psychic Influence

Chapter Six

Silent Psychic Influence

The Oriental Telepathy Techniques presented in the previous Chapter will be very helpful in developing your telepathic abilities.

Practice frequently bringing in quantities of prana to yourself via Rhythmic Breathing. And practice Crystal Gazing to increase your power of visualization. Make use of the formula of Visualization, Affirmation, Projection.

The forms of telepathy previously considered are objective in nature; experiments in thought transference between transmitter and percipient in which both are aware of the performance.

Silent Psychic Influence is the performance of telepathy with a major difference. In Silent Psychic Influence, the affirmation and the accompanying projection of the visualized thought are performed silently without the actual knowledge of the percipient. It is a subtle form of telepathy and, once proficiency is obtained, it is very effective.

In Silent Psychic Influence, the thought is powerfully energized by prana that manifests an intense degree of vibration producing a 'thought form' in relation to the 'feeling' of the thought, which is projected into the subconscious phase of mind of the percipient.

It will be observed that this involves the principle that thought (as a form of energy) may be transmitted over space, just as speech and sight may be transmitted via the appropriate waves of radio and television. With regard to telepathy, eastern knowledge has long accepted this fact. It is a natural manifestation of Nature. Actually, thought travels through hyperspace, as when projected from *here* it is immediately *there*.

Thought projection in Silent Psychic Influencing is different from conventional telepathy, which usually requires a specific rapport between people. In Silent Psychic Influence there is no such attunement, and it is not just a thought that is projected, but a 'thought form' along a psychic path through space (hyperspace) set up between the transmitter (projector) and the percipient. In this, it is said in the Orient, there is an astral and / or ethereal form charged with prana, which travels unerringly to its mark.

In the performance of this manifestation the evolved telepathic transmitter sees the thought form in their mind. When such is created by visualization it is projected by the will of the transmitter, after being energized by prana, by means of thought and will. If this description of the modus operandi seems a little complicated, it is actually an easier form to perform than regulated experiments. It is Nature's way, and is readily performed once the knack has been acquired. Here is the technique.

Begin by recognizing this fact: when we say 'thoughts are things', we are expressing literal truth. Thoughts are a form of energy, and while thought is a tenuous thing, yet it is decidedly real. When thought is sent forth (transmitted) with power (energy) it carries with it an amount of prana that increases its strength, often producing startling effects. The prana vitalizes the thought making it a *living force*.

The effects of Silent Psychic Influence may subconsciously influence people who are in close contact; also people who are at a distance. The operation is the same. Distance has no meaning to thought.

In the performance of Silent Psychic Influence the transmitter holds a clear mental-picture of the person who is to be silently transmitted to, along with what is desired to be accomplished. In this, the transmitter establishes in their own chitta what they wish to occur in the chitta of the percipient. The Yogis instruct the projector must:

SEE (visualize)

FEEL (affirmation)

WILL (project)

the desired response *for* and *to* the percipient.

The mental attitude of such performance being absolute assurance in 'knowing' that the silent influence will be felt and followed. No questions asked – it is a definite KNOWING it will be so.

Conversely, if the mental image is weak in the transmitting chitta, its effects will be weak in the chitta of the recipient. Keep in mind; the process of Silent Psychic Influence is much like the process of electrical induction. What occurs in one field is transferred to the other. To this end, before you attempt Silent Psychic Influence you must create in your own mind a positive ideal that you wish to have reproduced in the mind of the percipient.

The first 'law' of Silent Psychic Influence is to have the whole thing clearly mapped out, and know clearly, definitely, and positively exactly what you want to have happen, and how the percipient is to respond. Your silent telepathic process is much like a stage director who moves the actors about the stage in accordance to the script that he or she has studied in advance.

Having so prepared the psychic path in advance, proceed on. This preparatory work will greatly increase the power of Silent Psychic Influence.

Those experienced with using this technique say it is best to think in terms of impulsion rather than compulsion over the percipient. Compulsion is a force from without, while impulsion is a force from within. Compulsion might make an enemy; impulsion makes a friend of an enemy.

The method is simple. Do not try to compel to do what you desire. Rather project the *wish to do* what you desire.

Learning how to perform and use telepathy in its various forms has definite value to your success in life.

Your strength and power is of the inner realm of mind, and remember the unspoken word is the most powerful – when you learn how to use it. 'The Voice of the Silence' is the soundless sound prevailing over all verbalized speech. As it is written in the archives of the East:

> *"The silence is the workshop of the master telepathist; in it the great work is done; the rest is just materialization of that which has already been accomplished."*

Distant Thought Influencing

The second phase of Silent Psychic Influence is working with people at a distance. This phenomenon is no stranger to the West, as various kinds of 'absent treatments' are well known. Practitioners often report better results over a distance than when the treatment is given up close. Practitioners usually use the term 'treat' in connection with an illness, which sometimes tends to step on medical toes.

I use the term in the sense of *influence* in this text.

To benefit from your influence a distant person is a telepathic manifestation. You simply project to the person a picture-of-thought of personal well-being, well charged with prana, just as though he or she was with you in person. The better you can sense the actual psychic presence of the other person, the more fully will the psychic channel develop between you and the percipient, for the benefit of the latter.

Psychic channel development, in which you cause the distant person to be psychically present, may be achieved in several ways, e.g. producing a telepathic connection; visualizing the person as being present; making a telescoping viewing as though seeing the distant person through a telescope. It is possible to visualize the person in the crystal ball. Refer to Chapter Five and make use of those instructions.

A process that will assist you in establishing a psychic channel with a distant individual is to make use of what the Yogis call the 'Astral Tube'.

The Astral Tube is frequently employed for distant viewing. It consists of forming a tube-like, 'cleared path' psychically created in the akasha, enabling a free passage of the projected thought-form. The Astral Tube is a visualized creation that some say is a big help for making telepathic connections with a distant person.

Believe it or not!

A so-called successful establishment of psychic channel connection with the distant person, either with or without the Astral Tube results in a peculiar feeling of nearness with the individual. As you practice, you will come to recognize the experience. As you have learned, distance has no meaning to thought.

Time and space are nonexistent in the realm of thought. And never look upon telepathy as being something mystical. It may be supernormal, but it's most certainly not supernatural.

Chapter Seven

Yogi Mental Broadcasting

Chapter Seven

Yogi Mental Broadcasting

"Mental Broadcasting = Noisy Telepathy"

This is an Eastern technique. It is silent yet noisy, as it is the form of telepathy that influences a group or crowd with similar interests. I have named it 'Noisy Telepathy'.

A group or crowd with similar interest/purpose is very susceptible to telepathy.

Yoga acclaims that telepathy cannot only project one-to-one, but can be mentally broadcast over a large area simultaneously. Noisy Telepathy is received by those minds that are tuned for its reception. Generally speaking it is mass acceptable via 'The Law of Mental Attraction'.

The Law of Mental Attraction operates in the direction of 'thought contagion' – in the direction of attracting to each other person whose mental sentiment attitudes are attuned to the same psychic wavelength.

The mutual attraction of Noisy Telepathy manifests on the same general wavelength in two basic ways:

1. It attracts the percipient to the transmitter.

2. It attracts the transmitter to the percipient.

Thus, it may be said to generate a mental union of the group or crowd.

Whichever happens to be the line of least resistance in the way of thoughts, feelings and desires will be the line of telepathic attraction in response to a basic harmony (rapport). This is Mental Broadcasting.

Everyone, everywhere, in every situation sets into operation this form of telepathy. It is often accomplished spontaneously and with little definite purpose or direction, except when caught up in thought contagion.

As an example, the person sending forth continually gloomy and depressing thought vibrations will be found to attract people and things of a corresponding type.

Conversely, the person sending forth thought vibrations of a helpful and encouraging sort will be found to attract people and things of a corresponding cheerful type. In relation to telepathic influencing of a group or crowd such remains, and increases in response to the mental susceptibility of the group or crowd.

This telepathic principle works both ways: it attracts us and it repels us.

Noisy Telepathy can produce truly magical effects when used purposefully and constructively. The modus operandi is for the transmitter to deliberately plan the mental broadcast. Form the basis of Yogi Mental Broadcasting into clear mental-pictures showing precisely what is desired to be accomplished. Let it constitute a mental command.

Broadcast the call … and the call will be answered. When you perform Noisy Telepathy the results you put into operation will frequently even surprise yourself; sometimes so much so as to seem almost supernatural.

It is important that you appreciate this point; nothing is ever supernatural but is supernormal. Unless you plainly understand the natural character of these phenomena, you will fail to have faith in Nature's telepathic powers. Remember, children having faith that they *can* is why they are so successful in using telepathy.

It is held in Yoga that the everywhere-present and everywhere-active are the universal principles of akasha, prana, and creative mind These three principles are held to be immanent and present in everything throughout the Universe. Also, it is held there is no mindless thing in Nature. The Yoga teaching further expounds that everything is conscious to the degree of being exactly what it is.

There seems to exist a correlation between thoughts and things; a connection or rapport between them that causes them to move and act as the result of the direction of thought. Telepathy is the direction of thoughts, and thoughts are things.

To achieve what you want to achieve, to control the group or crowd, via telepathy, send out the Yogi Broadcasting Call. The Eastern teachings were not intended merely for past ages; they are as useful and powerful now in the 21st century, as ever they were.

Chapter Eight

The Telepathy of Love

Chapter Eight

The Telepathy of Love

Love attraction is a potent form of spontaneous telepathy. Love is worldwide, in both the East and the West. It is interesting to get the Eastern viewpoint.

In Yoga, love is perceived as a great cosmic law of attraction and activity. It is mental with deep feeling that makes it telepathic. Its influence is found throughout all Nature. The very word love is oriental in origin, being derived from the ancient Sanskrit term 'lubh', meaning craving. Love is the Yin and Yang of the universe. The more deeply you feel love the more telepathic you become.

There is a telepathic attraction of love to be found between all different things, inorganic as well as organic. Even in the scientific laboratory the love of atoms is recognized, and the science of physics now perceives that all matter is composed of minute particles which possess opposite qualities which strongly suggest the respective ideas of masculine and feminine. Science calls it charm.

Without the telepathic attraction of love, all of Nature's creative work would perish and never be renewed. The old classic is so very true, 'Tis love that makes the world go round' and keeps it going.

As Emerson expresses it, "We are made alive and kept alive by the power of love". It is a fact of Nature that the will to live is really the 'will to love'. Nature is the back of the love instinct in every way.

Love-influence is one of the most potent forms of psychic influence, and psychic influence is telepathy. Like the power of electricity, which is able to arouse by induction a similar state from one magnetic field to another, so the telepathic love vibration is capable of arousing by induction a similar rate of vibration within the subconsciousness of another. This is 'love-energy', which is the storage battery of telepathy. Love-energy is like a bolt of lightning seeking instinctively a point to strike. This is sex-magnetism.

Yoga has long recognized this subtle form of sex-magnetism. It is claimed in the East to be a form of prana, colored with strong-emotion vibrations.

Sex-magnetism when combined with love-energy is very important to the successful performance of telepathy.

The manifesting and expressing of the Telepathy of Love is a special form of application of the combined principles of visualization, affirmation and projection. By combining such with sex-magnetism, a most powerful telepathic influence is generated. The more you have love in your heart the greater master of telepathy you will be.

Want to be a most successful Mindreading Performer, as you will learn in Part Two of this Encyclopedia?

If you do, feel the same love in your heart for your audience as the great magician, Howard Thurston. Standing behind the front curtain before his show began Howard used to bounce vigorously up and down generating energy in his body, while exclaiming,

"I love my audience! I love my audience! I love my audience!"

Chapter Nine

Telepathy Research Then and Now

Chapter Nine

Telepathy Research Then and Now

Telepathy has such glamor to it that one tends to be less cautious in the investigation of the phenomena in the hope of showing striking results. The study of telepathy is of such importance to human relations that it calls for serious scientific study to remove it from the realm of fantasy.

It would be remiss in my telling of experiments with telepathy if I did not include this chapter expressing that the cold eye of science (the scientific attitude) must be turned upon the investigation of this colorful subject. How important this is stands out clear and sharp when comparing it with the early intrigue of the far less glamorous rock-solid subject of Geology. There is sardonic humor in this comparison.

It is salutary sometimes to reflect how recent is the growth of our scientific cosmos, and how brief an interval separates it from the chaos which went before. This may be seen even in sciences that deal with matters of common observation. Among material phenomena, the facts of Geology are assuredly not especially calculated to excite people's curiosity or impress their imagination. Yet the origin of the organic remains embedded in the rocks has indeed formed a subject of speculation ever since the days of Aristotle. It was suggested that they were formed by the plastic forces of Nature. Medieval astrologers ascribed their formation to planetary influences. And these hypotheses, with the alternative view of the Church, that fossil bones and shells were relics of the Mosaic Deluge, appear to have satisfied the learned of Europe until the time of Voltaire, who reinforced the rationalistic position, as he conceived it, by the suggestion that the shells, at any rate, had been dropped from the hats of pilgrims returning from the Holy Land.

Werner and Hutton were even then preparing to elucidate the cause of stratification and the genesis of the igneous rocks. Curvier, in the next generation, demonstrated the essential analogies of the fossils found in the Paris basin with living species. Agassiz was to investigate the relation of fossil fishes to show the growth and spread of organized knowledge. And still it was possible for a pious Scotsman to ascribe the origin of mountain chains to a cataclysm that, after the fall of Man, had broken up and distorted the once symmetrical surface of the Earth; for a Dean of York to essay bringing the Medieval theory up to date and prove that the whole series of geological strata, with their varied organic remains, were formed at the time of Noah's flood; and for another English reverend to warn his congregation against any sacrilegious meddling with the arena of rocks, because they belonged to the Creator, being storehouses of His celestial treasures.

If the rock-solid subject of Geology can cause such a mishmash, how much more can the subject of telepathy cause a roar of mumbo jumbo?

In its history, telepathy has gone through all manner of mysterious associations. Ghost and warning dreams have been matters of popular belief and interest since the earliest of times, and are known to all races from the most primitive to the most modern. Also, telepathy has become mixed up with witchcraft and spiritualism. All these associations have placed an aura of the mysterious about the subject, and almost every conjuror in the world has added imitated demonstrations of telepathy and mindreading in their shows.

No serious and organized attempt at investigating telepathy was made until 1882, when the Society of Psychical Research was founded in London, under the presidency of Professor Henry Sidgwick. He and his colleagues were pioneers in telepathic research, and such research has continued on into our current technological age.

But the forces of superstition and charlatanry, to which telepathy has for so long belonged, have bequeathed an unfortunate legacy to those who would colonize it in the name of Science. However, the appetite for the marvelous is not easily restrained. Careful scientific research of the subject is very much needed, as old habits of inaccuracy, of magnifying the proportion of things, of intertwining surmises with facts, cannot be eradicated without most careful discipline. Indeed, to one scientist those dangers seemed so serious that he warned the Society of Psychical Research against the risk of stimulating inborn tendencies of superstition by even the semblance of inquiry into such matters as telepathy. Truly, the clue to the interpretation of these most striking mental phenomena, since they occur for the most part spontaneously, is not without complication.

However, we are today living in a technological age, and this difficulty is growing less serious as more people who have received their training in other branches of science are attracted to the inquiry. The serious study of the phenomena of telepathy requires the best of minds, as so insidious in such investigation is the working of imagination, so untrustworthy is the memory, so various are the sources of error in human testimony, that it is obvious that much care must be applied to the academic research of telepathy.

Meanwhile, this *Secrets of Stage Mindreading* makes use of the UNKNOWN and the MYSTERIOUS to produce a most effective show. Stage Hypnotism also has these qualities, which is why telepathy and hypnotism blend so well.

Mysterious? Thought provoking? You bet!

MAKES A GREAT SHOW!

Part Two

How to Perform REAL Mindreading

Chapter Ten

Introduction to REAL Mindreading

Chapter Ten

Introduction to REAL Mindreading

Practice! Practice! Practice!

If you practice REAL Mindreading you will even amaze yourself at what you can do.

REAL Mindreading is psychic perception. Psychic perception is TELEPATHY. Can you do it? Of course you can. You do it often without even being aware that you do it. Children, such as the Creery children[2] often do it best, because they have not been told they can't.

Psychic means that REAL Mindreading is a form of inner perception. It comes in on its own as intuition. Just freely allow whatever comes in to become conscious to your awareness.

Mental flashes of telepathy often appear in visualized form. Every journey starts with taking the first step. The first step in becoming a masterful performer of telepathy and/or mindreading comes with the practice of learning how to effectively VISUALIZE.

[2] *Chapter One: Proof of Telepathy.*

Chapter Eleven

Developing Visualization Time

Chapter Eleven

Developing Visualization Time

To increase your power of visualization, practice often the 'Ladder of Colors' that is given in this Chapter.

In the practice of Yoga it is held that the spinal column provides an invisible channel in its center called the 'sushumna'. On either side of the sushumna flows a current of prana (vitality of life) of positive and negative nature – the two currents passing through the substance of the spinal cord.

The current, which flows on the right side is called 'pingul' and is the positive current. The current that flows on the left side is called 'ida' (pronounced ee-daa) and is the negative current. Spaced along these psychic energy channels in specific parts of the body are special energy centers called 'chakras'. The term chakra, in definition, means wheel, disc, or whirling-around object that is stimulated into activity by rising psychic energy (termed kundalini) ascending the channel of the sushumna. It is claimed there are seven main chakra centers spaced along the channel of the sushumna. The chakras are listed below in ascending order:

1. The MULADHARA. The lowest chakra located in the base of the spine.

2. The SVADHISTHANA. The second chakra, located on the spinal column in the region of the reproductive organs.

3. The MANIPURA. The third chakra, located on the spinal column in the region of the solar plexus.

4. The ANAHATA. The fourth chakra, located on the spinal column in the region of the heart.

5. The VISUDDUA. The fifth chakra, located on the spinal column in the region of the throat.

6. The AJANA. The sixth chakra, located in the region of the pineal gland within the head. (Frequently referred to as 'the third eye'.)

7. The SAHASTRARA. The seventh chakra, located at the top (crown) of the head. (Frequently referred to as 'the thousand petaled lotus'.)

Each chakra is associated with a specific color, which when visualized is said to produce a vibratory frequency that stirs into activity the operation of the chakra associated with it. The colors are:

RED   stimulating to the first chakra
ORANGE   stimulating to the second chakra
YELLOW   stimulating to the third chakra
GREEN   stimulating to the fourth chakra
BLUE   stimulating to the fifth chakra
VIOLET   stimulating to the sixth chakra
WHITE   stimulating to the seventh chakra

The color *white* is used as a cosmic connection (often forming an aura of protection about the user). When these colors are visualized, in sequence, they appear to increase perception, which is important to the performance of REAL Mindreading.

The Ladder of Colors method

Sit in a comfortable chair with your hands resting loosely in your lap. Rest your feet flat on the floor. Now, relax and take a deep breath. Exhale slowly. Do it again but this time while inhaling visualize the color WHITE (the color of the Sahastrara chakra) coming into nostrils and filling the lungs with WHITE LIGHT – entering your body and spreading throughout your entire nervous system. Just sit quietly with eyes closed. Breathe comfortably feeling WHITE LIGHT forming an aura of purity about yourself. Visualize it as a beautiful experience.

Rest a few moments.

Now, starting at the base of the spine, go up the Ladder of Colors. With eyes still closed, visualize – within your mind – the color RED. Fill your head with the color RED. Visualize RED, in anyway you please: a red rose, a red apple, anything that is RED.

Rest a few moments.

Now, go up to the color ORANGE. Visualize the color ORANGE within your mind. See ORANGE anyway you please: a bowl of oranges, a glass of orange juice, a Buddhist monk in an orange robe. Visualize the color ORANGE anyway you please. See ORANGE with your mind's eye inside your head.

> Rest a few moments.

Now, go up the ladder to the color YELLOW. Visualize YELLOW. Fill your head with YELLOW. Picture it anyway you please: the yellow yoke of an egg, the yellow center of a daisy. A blazing yellow sun.

> Rest a few moments.

Now, go up the ladder of your spinal column, and visualize the color GREEN. See GREEN inside your head. Fill your head with GREEN. See GREEN as you wish: green grass, green leaves, a glowing green emerald.

> Rest a few moments.

Now, go up the ladder and visualize the color BLUE. See BLUE clearly with your mind's eye: a blue sky, a blue lake. Use whatever image you like to visualize the color BLUE.

> Rest a few moments.

Finally, go up the Ladder of Colors and reach the color VIOLET. Visualize VIOLET LIGHT filling your head. Possibly, mentally see a bunch of violets, anything you wish as long as it fills your mind with the color VIOLET.

Allow yourself to rest longer, submerged in the color VIOLET. Let VIOLET be as a mist that you drop yourself into. Rest as long as you please, submerged in VIOLET. Possibly even drop off to sleep. Come back to wakefulness any time you wish.

Practice performing The Ladder of Colors any time and as often as you wish. It trains you in what comes into your mind in visualized form. It increases your sensitivity. It advances your perception. It soars your skill of performing REAL Mindreading.

Chapter Twelve

Developing Body Awareness

Chapter Twelve

Developing Body Awareness

"Mind and Body act each upon the other in a continuous circling of both conscious and subconscious reaction."

In one's process of living, the mind continuously affects the body and the body continuously affects the mind – both on conscious and subconscious levels.

As REAL Mindreading (both contact and non-contact) functions on the subconscious level, the more you learn about the subconscious phase of mind, the better mindreader you will be.

In the previous Chapter, you were given a technique to increase your subconscious power of visualization and activate the chakra centers. The Ladder of Colors is decidedly subconscious.

In this Chapter you will be given a technique to subconsciously advance body awareness. The technique is called 'Leetha' and hails from Indonesia, where many natives practice it daily, for hours at a time.

The Leetha Method

Sit in a chair, extend your arms in front of you, and start shaking your hands vigorously. Shake them in any direction, any way they want to go. Just shake them wildly, in absolute freedom. You start with effort, but soon the shaking will become effortless, and it will seem to occur almost by itself. As you do this, allow your mind to grow calm and experience yourself becoming the shaking. The time will come when it seems that it is no longer your hands that are shaking, rather it is YOU who is shaking both inside and out.

When you become the shaking rather than just doing the shaking, you will begin to feel yourself filling with energy; an energy that somehow seems both mental and physical, at one and the same time. After you have become the shaking of your hands, and have had enough of this activity, relax your hands in your lap, and rest a bit. This is your introduction to performing Leetha – now get down to the nitty-gritty.

Stand erect, close your eyes, and allow your whole body to vibrate. You will find this easy to do as you have already started the energy flowing throughout your body.

So, now just allow your whole body to become energy, allowing your body to melt and dissolve its boundaries. Just stand relaxed, loose, and natural. You do not have to do anything; you are simply there waiting for something to happen; all you have to do is cooperate with it and allow it. The cooperation should not become too direct, it should not be a pushing; it should remain just an allowing. You will find that your body will start making movements on its own. Which movements it makes depends on you; everyone is different.

Possibly your head will twitch and your body will start shaking in different ways. Just allow your body to take on the shaking freely, and shake any way it wants to go.

Possibly your body will make subtle movements like a little dance, your hands move, your legs move, seemingly on their own, and your entire body starts performing subconscious movements. Sometimes the experience is quite amazing, as it is subconscious. *All you have to do is just allow it to happen.*

The energy is very subtle, so do not resist it. Just allow it to develop on its own, and as it does, THINK of the vibration of your body being the energy of the Cosmos coming into you.

When you have had enough of these automatic movements of your body *just stop*. You can stop any time you please. Now, stand still with your eyes closed and breathe deeply while directing the energy towards your brain. Visualize your brain glowing like a ball of light (energy), and from the brain passing through every nerve of your body permeating every fibre of your BEING.

You will recognize in this the subconscious combining of mind visualization and body awareness – attributes importance to the performance of REAL Mindreading.

Use your imagination in doing this. In your mind's eye, see the energy you have brought into your body flowing throughout your entire body. You are alive with energy. Never be afraid to use your imagination. If you want to read minds, imagine that you can.

REAL Mindreading operates like a 'mental radio' – the person sending the thoughts is the transmitter and the person receiving the thoughts is the receiver. Like radio or TV, the more the frequencies are attuned to each other, the better the communication (reception). Attunement in mindreading is called rapport.

The dictionary describes rapport as a relationship marked by harmony, conformity, accord, or affinity.

In relation to mindreading, take two people and try this process:

Face each other and both violently shake their hands together, as a mutual action. In doing this, the transmitter holds the thought that what he (or she) wishes to transmit is visualized in their mind, while the receiver opens his (or her) mind to be receptive of the visualized thought.

This mutual shaking of hands creates vibrations (frequencies) forming rapport between the individuals. The accomplishment of mindreading is just around the corner.

Chapter Thirteen

Contact and Non-Contact Mindreading

Chapter Thirteen

Contact and Non-Contact Mindreading

There are two types of mindreading demonstrations that can be presented. Contact Mindreading is the most practical to use for public shows. Non-Contact Mindreading is effective for social diversions.

Contact Mindreading

Contact Mindreading is accomplished when the transmitter of thoughts grips the arm or hand of the receiver, which affords mini-physical responses to the thought to be subtly conveyed to the receiver, leading to successfully accomplishing the thought-of act. In learning to perform mindreading it is best to first master Contact Mindreading, which frequently leads to mastering the performance of Non-Contact Mindreading.

Although it is unlikely that he would take credit for it, the basic explanation of Contact Mindreading was given by the famous psychologist, William James, who advanced the psychological/physiological concept that every thought in the mind produces an accompanying unconscious muscular response in the body. James termed it 'ideomotor action' and regarded it as a subconscious mental phenomenon.[3] Magicians have called it 'muscle reading'. Actually, it is a subtler mind to mind communication than is speech. It takes practice and skill to perform this form of mental communication. Few have mastered it, so demonstrations of Contact Mindreading can prove very mystifying.

In a typical demonstration of Contact Mindreading, in a theatrical format, unbeknown to the performer an object is hidden in the audience by a volunteer, who is known as the *thought transmitter*. The performer is recalled and blindfolded, being the thought-receiver in the demonstration.

[3] *James, William, PhD. Psychology pub. Henry Holt & Co., 1980*

95

The transmitter grasps the wrist of the receiver, and step by step concentrates on the receiver moving to the spot where the object is hidden and discovering it. Thus, silently leading the transmitter, the performer (receiver) moves through the audience and locates the hidden object. The effect on the spectators is remarkable.

John R. Brown is considered the originator of public performances for this kind of Mindreading. He initiated the presentation in 1873. He was a master mentalist whose expertise was the inspiration for the development of yet another master, in the person of Washington Irving Bishop. Bishop, in turn, contributed to the work of the famous magician, Stuart Cumberland. These men featured Contact Mindreading in their shows and gained international reputations.

Down through the years there have been acclaimed performers of mental magic who have included demonstrations of this form of Mindreading in their programs: Andrew Seymor, Paul Alexandra, Hellstrom, Lucy de Gentray, DeWaldoza, Dunninger, Polgar, George Newman, Kreskin, and other magical stars have added to their professional stature by mastering the skill.

Non-Contact Mindreading

This second form of mindreading is like 'mental radio' communication. To really understand it, one must marvel at the capacities of our biocomputer brain.

We live currently in a space and time where computers are everywhere, but we have within our head the greatest computer of all. A good computer on your desk has some 800 million transistor connections. Your biocomputer brain has 1000 billion connections, and one of its functions is telepathy.

Telepathic energy is the product of thought. Every thought produces an electric like (chemical type) discharge in the brain, and an electric discharge produces a wave. A thought wave is much like a radio wave, but far more subtle. It can transmit through space from one person to another, irrespective of distance.

Willpower is not used to push the thought; *will* is only used to form the thought, and place it in the center of the mind where it is visualized. This means the transmitted mental picture of what is wanted to occur in the mind of the receiver is visualized as ripples of thought occurring in the transmitter's 'lake of mind' (called chitta in India) – then similar mental pictures form in the mind of the other person.[4]

Non-Contact Mindreading (telepathy) is the transmission of mental waves or currents. The brain of the transmitter, aroused by active will, sends a thought current or wave, through space, to the receiver's nervous system, spontaneously influencing their actions.

Such is the modus operandi of the inner working of the mental radio, in other words, Non-Contact Mindreading. In this form, the receiver will find that when they go to work, say in the search of a hidden object, they will literally forget the transmitter.

[4] *Chapter Five: Oriental Telepathy Techniques.*

Chapter Fourteen

Performing Contact Mindreading

Chapter Fourteen

Performing Contact Mindreading

"The best way to learn to do anything is to start right in and learn how to do it. Then do it."

Prelude to Contact Mindreading

Human communication is based on mind to mind contact. Mind to mind contact is mindreading. It takes three forms.

1. Verbalized thoughts/Speech

It is so common it's not regarded as mysterious. Yet it is very powerful. Through constant use, words have become unconscious triggers to action – which is to say they express our feelings consciously and subconsciously. Experiment and observe.

Think LOVE … then speak out loud to yourself, "Love", and you will commence feeling love energy. Think HATE … then speak out loud, "Hate", and you will commence feeling hate energy. Try it with other emotionally charged words, such as envy, anger, jealousy, greed, etc. and you will feel the specified emotion rising within you. Why? Because the response to verbalized speech (words) has become *conditioned* in your mind through repeated use. Don't ever underestimate the power of words. Try HAPPINESS and see what happens.

It has been said, "The right word spoken at the right time in the right way can move the world". And remember it is the thought behind the word that is important. The more familiar you can get with 'feeling', the better mindreader you will be when you learn how to perform Contact Mindreading.

2. Contact Mindreading

This form of mind to mind communication is based on William James' Ideomotor Action. In other words, it's words spoken silently through body language. It is mysterious, for most people are not even aware that it is there to be perceived. Learn the art, and you will become an expert MINDREADER.

3. Non-Contact Mindreading

This is direct mind to mind communication. It is the ultimate form of mindreading (telepathy). Contact Mindreading and Non-Contact Mindreading closely resemble the two classes of telegraphic systems, i.e. the wire system and the wireless system. These forms often dovetail together.

Performing Contact Mindreading

Once you master Contact Mindreading you will have an amazing entertainment feature you can present that is fascinating. It's great show business. As you become proficient, you can design your own show and present the routines you wish to present. Success begets success, and with success comes confidence.

Begin by understanding the psychological/physiological principle of IDEOMOTOR ACTION, which is that every thought of motion held in the mind produces an automatic (unconscious) muscular response in the body, in the direction of the thought. It is so slight as to be invisible, but it is there. You can immediately gain an understanding of this principle with this pendulum experiment:

> Tie a finger ring to the end of a six-inch length of thread, making a pendulum. Extend your right arm and grip the top end of the thread, allowing the ring to dangle down. You are holding a pendulum.

> Now, think consciously of holding your right hand absolutely still while looking at the pendulum, and *thinking* of it beginning to swing back-and-forth from right to left. It will start swinging in the direction of your thoughts.

> Now, think of the ring stopping and commence swinging round and round in a circle. It will stop, and then respond by swinging in a circle.

You have demonstrated Ideomotor Action upon which Contact Mindreading is based. The conscious thought of direction movement (as a feeling of the movement) produced an unconscious very subtle muscular response to the thought.

This is nonverbalized body language that the receiver (YOU) must respond to.

The transmitter directs the thought, while gripping the receiver's wrist (depending on the method used) and *thinks* of the receiver moving in the direction of the thought. All the receiver has to do is be passive and follow the impulses he or she senses telling them mentally where to go and what to do.

Is it mindreading?

Of course it is, for it is the perception of unspoken thought.

As you use unsolicited volunteers (either men or women) directly from the audience to be transmitters in your mindreading experiments, the volunteers must be sincere, follow your instructions, and want the experiments to be successful as much as you do. It is a privilege to participate in a mindreading demonstration. It will be remembered for a lifetime. Many in the audience will clamor for the opportunity. It is well to start each demonstration by breathing together in unison for a few moments. This creates rapport.

The demonstration having been decided upon between transmitter and receiver, say in locating an object hidden somewhere in the theatre … have yourself blindfolded, just stand and wait while the transmitter hides the object (anyone can hide the object just as long as the transmitter knows where it is hidden). Returning to stand by your side, the transmitter grips your wrist, and mentally directs you – step by step – where to go to find the hidden object. You must respond to his or her thoughts, which makes it mindreading.

To understand what is meant by step by step, understand that the transmitter never thinks of the end result of the experiment, but takes you mentally along gradually until the end of the experiment is finally reached. Thus, step by step, you are mentally guided along your mindreading journey. Let's consider an example:

> A comb is borrowed and given to a person seated in the tenth row along the aisle. The party hides the comb in his or her left coat pocket. You have no idea where the comb is hidden, but the transmitter does.

The test starts …

While gripping your wrist, the transmitter thinks if you are to start moving to the right or left. Move as you feel an impulse to move. Sometimes you may start out in the wrong direction. When this happens, stop, wait for the corrected impulse and move accordingly. This accomplished, the transmitter next thinks of you going down the theatre aisle. The transmitter will think, "STOP" when the tenth row is reached.

Next the transmitter will think on which side of the aisle you are to turn.

Wait for the impulse and turn in that direction. You will sense a feeling of satisfaction when you do things correctly.

Next, the transmitter may tell you verbally to extend your free left hand. As you do so, you will feel an impulse to lower your hand and touch the person you have reached. Do so.

The transmitter will then think, "Lower your hand and reach into the left coat pocket". Do so, and you will find the comb hidden there. You will feel a definite impulse to reach into the pocket. If you are correctly interpreting, the transmitter will go freely with you in this movement. If incorrect, you will sense a slight resistance ... then, wait a moment for the impulse to come again. When corrected, the transmitter will go freely with your movement as you reach into the pocket and find the comb.

The hidden object has been discovered by following mental directions from the transmitter to the receiver. Contact Mindreading is based the art of *feeling*, and with practice the responses become sensitive and automatic. In time, you will get so good at it that it will seem you are dragging the transmitter behind you as you advance to the objective goal.

Performing Contact Mindreading takes practice. It is a skill not many people have. In fact, most people haven't the slightest idea how you do it. It seems unfathomable. It belongs to the magician's realm.

Chapter Fifteen

The Ormond McGill Method

Chapter Fifteen

The Ormond McGill Method

In my own performance, I have found a simple way to instruct the transmitter to mentally guide the receiver to successfully perform each Contact Mindreading experiment.

Do this ...

Tell the transmitter to tell you mentally – step by step – the instructions of where you are to go and what you are to do. They speak these instructions *silently* to themselves within their head, just the same as they would tell them to you in conventional verbal speech.

For example, if the transmitter wishes the receiver to do this or that, they simply present these instructions, precisely as they would give you instructions in verbal conversation. While mentally giving the instructions they should *feel* themselves performing the instructions that they are mentally speaking to you (feel the movements suggested by the instructions).

The transmitter grips the wrist of the receiver while this is done. Always make contact when performing Contact Mindreading.

Practice this in private with a friend and see how well it works. The directions given in this manner by the transmitter will be felt, via the contact, as impulses from the receiver of where to go and what to do, precisely as if they were spoken verbally.

Simple. It works. All kinds of Contact Mindreading demonstrations can be presented by this internal telling by the transmitter telling the receiver (YOU) where to go and what to do.

Just remember when you tell the transmitter how to transmit their thoughts, that while they are speaking silently to themselves inside their head what the receiver is to do, they must allow themselves to feel they are performing exactly what they are mentally telling the receiver to perform. The impulse will come through the contact on transmitter's hand upon receiver's wrist. Often it will seem like a spontaneous impulse to do what is felt.

Understand ...

As an example, if the transmitter speaks mentally to themselves, "Move to the right", they must allow themselves to *feel* themselves moving to the right. They do not actually physically move to the right, but they mentally feel themselves moving to the right, and the receiver will pick up the impulse to physically move to the right.

Using this method, you can perform all kinds of Contact Mindreading experiments.

I REPEAT: Practice well in private before you perform in public.

Chapter Sixteen

Practicing Contact Mindreading

Chapter Sixteen

Practicing Contact Mindreading

All the things you have learned and done, such as increasing your power of visualization, body awareness, and instructing the transmitter to internally speak his or her mental directing thoughts, contribute to your skill in Contact Mindreading. Now, we will get down to the actual business of experimenting with experiencing how to do it, and actually start doing it as performance demonstrations.

Producing a GREAT SHOW is the goal. If you are a successful Stage Hypnotist and have a great show, you can make your show even greater by adding some experiments in Contact Mindreading. Often demonstrations in Contact Mindreading are used as a prelude to the Hypnotism Show. They form an initial contact with your audience, show your skill as a performer, advance your prestige, and cause the spectators to willingly join you on stage to participate in your hypnotic demonstrations, as they come to personally know you as a performer and admire that you can read minds.

Practice makes perfect

Everyone, for better or for worse, can learn how to perform Contact Mindreading, as everyone has a mind. However, it takes talent to do it well. Mindreading is an art form. It is like singing. Everyone can learn the rudiments of singing, but only a few reach the concert stage. If you become a MASTER, it can bring you fame and fortune.

We will now get down to the nitty gritty of performing Contact Mindreading, even if we have to repeat a bit.

Mindreading feats depend upon *Will* and *Concentration* on the part of the TRANSMITTER (volunteer) and upon *Receptivity* and *Passivity* on the part of the RECEIVER (performer). Instructions will be given for the best performance of both so that the proper harmony and rapport conditions may be established. So get busy and practice.

Development exercises

Practice privately with a few friends, who are as interested in learning mindreading as you are. Through practice you will gain confidence and polish your performance. Then, when ready, the time will come for you to appear before an audience to present demonstrations in mindreading with confidence and polish.

Ready, set, GO!

Select one of your sympathetic friends to play the part of the transmitter, while you assume the role of the receiver. The practice best begins by establishing rapport, between yourself and your transmitter by means of Rhythmic Breathing.

In the dictionary, rapport is defined as relationship, conformity, sympathetic accord, harmony between individuals. Developing harmonious vibration with the transmitter is important to successful mindreading. To become a successful mindreader you must learn how to quickly establish this rapport with your transmitter volunteer, in performance.

In performing Rhythmic Breathing between two people, both do this together:

- inhale a breath for six counts

- hold the breath for three counts

- exhale the breath for six counts

- breathe in this rhythm together a few times, and *vibrational harmony* quickly develops between you.

A half dozen such breaths together will be sufficient. Practice this Rhythmic Breathing, and start each demonstration with it.

Another method I have found to develop rapport between you at the start of each demonstration is to think in terms of bringing in Cosmic Force to empower the experiment. For this:

The volunteer transmitter and receiver performer stand facing each other. Arms hang down by their sides, with hands out about ten inches from the body (hands must not touch the body). Both close their eyes, and they take three deep breaths together.

As the third breath is held they request out loud in unison, "We call upon the universe to bring cosmic energy into us to give us mutual Strength, Guidance, and Protection". Both then wait in silence and center their attention upon their hands. Remarkably, a form of cosmic energy does come in and seems to make the fingers tingle.

Imagination? Who knows, but it is a decidedly physical sensation. Use this method before each mindreading experiment. A strong rapport is developed. Somehow this incoming energy seems to empower the success of the mindreading experiments. Not necessary, of course, but sometime give it a try.

A prime requisite for a successful demonstration of Contact Mindreading is for the transmitter to know exactly what demonstration is to be performed, and have a clear *sense of direction* in their mind for the performance of the demonstration. So strongly is this done, that although they do not move, *they strongly feel the sensation of themselves moving in the direction of their thoughts*.

Begin by having the transmitter stand beside you in the center of the room. Close your eyes, or even better be blindfolded. Have them select mentally one corner of the room (which corner is entirely unknown to you). Then, have them concentrate upon that mentally elected corner, forgetting every other part of the room. Then, have the transmitter grasp your left hand with their right hand; you grasping their fingers in your hand and lifting the hand to your forehead. Hold the hand against the center to your forehead just above your eyes. This places the connection at the third eye center, known in India as 'The Eye of Shiva'.

Now, instruct them to *will* that you go to the corner of the room they have mentally selected, shutting out all other thoughts from their mind and *concentrating* their entire attention upon the projection of their *will*. In doing this, they must think of the direction of that corner, just as they would in wanting to walk to that corner themselves. They must not simply think 'that corner' – they must think 'there', as a sense of direction. They must *will* that you go there, carrying the words "Go there!" in their mind.

As the receiver, you must place yourself in a passive and receptive state of mind; willing and desirous of being mentally directed (led) by the *will* of the transmitter.

They are the active factor and you are the passive. It is the strength of their *will*, and the degree of your receptivity that makes the experiment a success.

Keep your eyes closed, even though you are blindfolded – it assists you maintain a passive state of mind – shutting out sights and even thought of sights.

Stand quiet for a few moments, awaiting impressions to come to you from the mind of the transmitter who is making the mental command to you, "Go there ... go to the corner of the room of which I am thinking". At the same time, they are *willing* that you "Go there".

After a few moments of passive and receptive waiting you will begin to feel an impulse to move forward. Obey this impulse and take the first step, which will not necessarily be in the direction of the selected corner. The idea of this first step is to *get started*. While you are taking the first step or two, you will start to feel the impulse move you in the direction of the selected corner. *Follow the impulse.* Move in the direction you sense you wish to go. Somehow you will find yourself swinging around to face the correct position.

Do not grow impatient. Just take your time, for remember you are just practicing; you are learning how to receive impressions. Advance one foot forward, hesitate, resting your weight on the ball of the other foot, and you will soon feel yourself being *compelled* to move in a certain direction, which will end by your moving towards the mentally selected corner of the room. Keep practicing, and you will soon become conscious of being directed by the *will* of the transmitter. Don't be disturbed by early failure. Just keep practicing, and soon you will get the knack.

It is difficult to describe the exact feeling you will experience but the practicing will soon make it clear to you. Follow the impulse to move as the impulse directs, and you will soon sense the mental command, "This way ... this way ... no, not that way but this way", until you will reach the desired spot, when you will sense the command, "That's right ... stop where you are ... this is the place". If you start to wander off in the wrong direction you will begin to feel the correcting impression, "This way ... this way I tell you to go". Allow yourself to passively receive and follow the mental commands that come in to move in the direction of the mental command.

As you practice, you will find the impulse growing stronger and stronger until you walk right into the selected corner. When you walk in the right direction you will feel the mental message, "Right. You are moving correctly. Right you are". When you walk in the wrong direction, you will feel the mental message saying, "No! No! Not that way. This way. Come along". These mental messages come in not so much as actual words of direction, but as impulses to move in the directions the words convey. *Mindreading is based on feelings*. Become sensitive to the feelings (impulses) and you will soon be performing successful mindreading. It is definitely mindreading you are doing, but since a physical contact is made between the transmitter and the receiver during the experiment, it is called Contact Mindreading.

With practice you will soon become quite sensitive to these guiding impulses and will respond to them almost automatically. Practice will soon so sharpen your inner perceptive faculties that you will often be able to move right off to the desired corner at once, sometimes actually running right to it, and dragging the transmitter after you!

Evaluating the transmitter

You will soon begin to notice there is quite a difference in the power of concentration on the part of different people acting as the transmitter. Some will be able to concentrate so forcibly that they will send you the message (impulse) clear and sharp, while others will send only a feeble and wavering message.

The more power of concentration the transmitter has, the stronger will be the message, which makes it easy for you to follow the impulses to move as you sense being mentally directed. In your practice it is well to work with different people acting as transmitters, so you become familiar with the different degrees of concentration you will work with. Learning to respond to all degrees of concentration is a mark of your advancing skill as a mindreader.

When you experience a transmitter who is sending only feeble messages, stop and tell them that they must exercise their *willpower* more. This often arouses a desire to concentrate more, as people like to feel they have strong willpower and they will begin sending you strong mental messages.

Another process that often works well to improve a feeble transmitter is to extend their arm out full length and hold it about the height of your eyes. In this way, they feel the strain and it arouses their will in order to hold it there. This seems to act in the direction of their sending sharper and clearer messages and impulses.

If the transmitter proves very unsatisfactory, substitute them for another. But as a rule this is not necessary. Most unsatisfactoriness arises from the fact that they do not fully understand just what is required of them to be a good transmitter. A bit of instruction as to how they are to *will* and *concentrate* will often correct difficulties. The transmitter will find that by *looking* towards the selected corner, they will be aided in concentrating their attention and directing their willpower. Most of all let your enthusiasm for the success of the experiment become equally the transmitter's enthusiasm for the success of the experiment.

When both the transmitter and the receiver cooperate, results can be outstanding.

Continue practicing

Practice this exercise of locating a mentally selected corner of the room in different rooms and with different transmitters until you can readily feel (sense) the impulse to go to the selected corner, any time and wherever the case may be.

In performing Contact Mindreading, always follow your impulses.

Mindreading is a skill, and the more you practice a skill the more skillful you become. PRACTICE MAKES PERFECT.

Chapter Seventeen

Contact Mindreading Exercises

Chapter Seventeen

Contact Mindreading Exercises

After you have grown proficient in locating the corners of rooms, then have the transmitter select other parts of the room, such as doors, mantels, windows, alcoves, projections, etc. Try a number of these mentally selected locations in turn, gaining a variety of experiences in responding to the impulses that come in. The same principle applies to finding all locations, as in finding a mentally selected corner of a room. All such practice advances your skill as a mindreader.

Since you are blindfolded, the transmitter must guard you from running into obstacles, such as furniture, etc. guiding you past them to avoid bruising yourself. You must impress upon the transmitter that in all mindreading experiments you perform together, you place yourself in their care with perfect confidence, so you may be completely unconcerned about such things.

You must keep your mind passive. Don't allow your mind to be distracted by outside things. Attend fully to the experiment you are performing.

Practice finding large objects

The next step in your developing skill of mindreading should be of finding large objects in the room, as mentally selected by the transmitter, e.g. chairs, tables, etc. Proceed as in your previous exercises. You need this for training. You will realize the importance of these early exercises when you eventually create a public show, and are called upon to find hidden objects, selected articles secreted under tables, on people, on furniture, etc.

If you can find selected chairs, obviously you will be able to find people seated in the chairs. Continue this exercise until you can readily find every piece of furniture in the room, and other large objects in the room WHEN THEY ARE THOUGHT OF BY THE TRANSMITTER.

Practice finding small objects

After mastering the foregoing exercise of mentally finding large objects, have the transmitter select some small articles, such as a book, vase, pencil on a table, etc.

Proceed in this practice of locating small objects, varying the objects and places, endeavoring to get as wide a range of experiences as possible. All such practice advances your expertise as a mindreader.

Practice finding hidden objects

After you have mastered the foregoing exercise have the transmitter take a small object, such as a watch, finger-ring, etc., and hide it in some part of the room. As you are blindfolded, you have not the slightest idea where it is hidden. Remain passive, and have the transmitter grip your wrist, while they direct you mentally – step by step – to where the object is hidden. You will feel the impulses come in to move you to where the object is hidden. It is no more difficult to find a hidden object than it is to find an object out in the open; it just takes a bit more mental instruction.

Have your transmitter give you great variety in this exercise. Have them place a key in a book, under a rug, behind a picture, in a table drawer, and similar hiding places. Then they grip your wrist and *concentrate* and *will* you to go to where the object is hidden. As long as the transmitter knows where the object is hidden, no object is hidden to you. In such experiments, they must give you the mental message, "UP, DOWN, TO THE RIGHT, TO THE LEFT", etc. While more detailed, the modus operandi is precisely the same, as their former, "GO THIS WAY", and so forth. You must train yourself to respond to these more subtle mental movement commands. It is no more difficult than finding a selected corner of room that has been thought of … just more detailed. This practice is very valuable to you, when you have to find objects in spectators' pockets, etc.

Practice finding a person

In a group, have a person mentally selected by the transmitter. Just as you did in your practice of finding a mentally selected corner of a room, find the general location of the person. Then, standing still, reach out your right hand and begin 'feeling about'. You will find that as your hand moves away from the right person you will feel a *drawing back* impression, whereas when you reach towards the right person you will feel an *urging forward* impression.

With practice you will soon be able to distinguish distinctly these mental impressions (impulses). Then, place your hand on the person in the center of the impression. If this is the wrong person, you will receive a mental impression of 'wrong' – in which case move your hand around until you feel the *urge impression*. When you feel it, immediately touch the person; you will receive an unmistakable impression of '*correct*' followed by an immediate leasing of the will-direction of the transmitter. You know you have succeeded. Practice this locating of a thought-of person over and over, until you can succeed in locating the person every time. It is important to your later public demonstrations.

Remarks on private practice

Practice. Practice. Practice these exercises until what they instruct becomes second nature to you. In time, you will find the mental commands to do this and that they come in almost as clearly as if the directions were spoken. What is interesting is that as you become more and more familiar with Contact Mindreading, Non-Contact Mindreading begins to activate. Contact Mindreading and Non-Contact Mindreading have a way of dovetailing together.

As each test in mindreading is successfully completed, you can sense, that while elated, the transmitter is relieved when, say, the hidden object is found. The relaxing of their mental tension may be distinctly felt.

In a nutshell, the rule for successful demonstrations of Contact Mindreading is to *always follow the line of the least resistance*. You will always receive resistance when you are not correct, and you will receive lack of resistance when you are correct. Learn to focus these impressions until they center positively and consistently on the same spot, and you will be correct.

Chapter Eighteen

Mindreading Show Routines

Chapter Eighteen

Mindreading Show Routines

An effective routine in relation to a show is to make what you do entertaining. That is showmanship. Showmanship is to get maximum effect out of what you do. In relation to mindreading, it is transforming experiment into entertainment. Remarkable as mindreading is, remember you are not conducting scientific research, you are presenting very personal ENTERTAINMENT.

The human mind has long been held as the citadel of personal privacy. When the mindreader shows that privacy can be invaded, the effect is startling – a Mindreading Show holds an audience glued to their seats. As entertainment, mindreading, just like hypnotism, is in a class by itself. In this chapter is an assemblage of effective routines you can do. Embellish them with your personal charisma and everyone will have a good time.

Every one of these effective routines is accomplished by mindreading skills you have learned how to perform.

The Floral Tribute

Have a bouquet of flowers on the table. Then select some young man in the audience to be your transmitter. He comes forward and joins you. You tell him to look over the audience and mentally select a lovely lady to whom he would like to give the flowers. He is to mentally direct you through the audience to find the beautiful woman of whom he is thinking. Quite a challenge to find one girl amongst a thousand people, and you don't even know who she is. You can do it, as long as the transmitter knows.

You pick up the bouquet and he grips your wrist while he *concentrates* and *wills* you – step by step – to make delivery of the flowers.

Down amidst the spectators you plunge, dragging the transmitter beside you. You find the lady, hand the bouquet to the young man who gives it to the girl. IT'S ENTERTAINMENT!

As you know from what you have learned, this routine is easy to do. Just use Contact Mindreading for finding a person.

The Marriage

Invite two large men to come on stage to make sure you cannot see or hear during this mindreading demonstration.

One man places his hands over your eyes, and the other places his hands over your ears. You are under control – obviously you cannot see or hear, but you can still speak.

You tell the audience to select two people in their midst – a young man and a young woman. Have them stand and come forward like a couple about to be married. Then a man is selected to play the role of minister. The three people then return to their seats in the audience. You have no idea where or who they are, but your transmitter does, as they have been watching all the time. The men release your eyes and ears, and stand aside. Keep them on the stage to join the cast – you can play mindreading as a full-stage production. The more you involve the audience in the feats, the more your show will be enjoyed. People like people, and all who volunteer are part of the audience itself.

IT'S AUDIENCE PARTICIPATION.

You are blindfolded.

The test is for you to first find the 'Minister' … then the 'Groom' … then the 'Bride'. The transmitter grips your wrist and you are on your way.

The routine plays as great theater. It's not difficult. Just a matter of locating people, as you have learned how to do in your private practicing.

These examples of Contact Mindreading show how the demonstrations may be dramatized to become very entertaining theater. The following outlines various mindreading feats upon which you can hang your own decorations.

The Hidden Knife Test

You stand before the audience and explain that when thought transference takes place between two people in direct mental communication, it is called mindreading. In mindreading, the person who sends the thought is known as the transmitter and the one who receives the thought is known as the receiver. You will demonstrate.

You request someone in the audience, who would like to experiment with mindreading, to volunteer to act as the transmitter in thought transference. The party comes up and joins you. They as the transmitter and you as the receiver perform The Hidden Knife Test.

You are blindfolded. The volunteer goes into the audience and borrows a pocketknife from someone. This done, you tell them to take the knife and give it to any person they wish. The person takes it, and puts it in a pocket. The knife is hidden. However, the transmitter knows exactly where it is.

Returning to the stage, the volunteer transmitter stands beside you, and grips your left wrist. You tell them to *concentrate* and *will* you to go out into the audience and find the knife. Step by step they are to mentally guide you.

You start out and lead the way, with the transmitter maintaining contact. They stand beside you as you move along, but you are the one who obviously is advancing according to the thoughts that come into you. The transmitter just goes where you lead.

Blindfolded into the audience you go until you reach the person who has the hidden knife.

There are a few moments pause, as your right hand gropes out. Suddenly your hand darts down into the person's pocket and brings forth the hidden knife. The test is a success.

As a Contact Mindreader, you know exactly how to do it.

The Hidden Ring Test

This test in mindreading is performed in a very similar way to the foregoing test. A volunteer borrows a ring from someone in the audience and hides it in some person's pocket. You are blindfolded while this goes on, and await the transmitter's return.

Standing by your side they *concentrate* and *will* you – step by step – to find the hidden ring. You go into the audience – leading the way with the transmitter lagging behind you and find the hidden ring.

This is the first half of the test.

Then …having found the hidden ring, you lead the transmitter back to the person from whom the ring was borrowed, and replace it on the finger where it belongs.

For drama in the presentation, borrow the ring from a woman who treasures her engagement ring.

The modus operandi for this test is the same as you have learned.

Sorting out the hats

You stand blindfolded. Let us say, "You are in the dark".

The transmitter goes into the audience to borrow six hats (men's and women's hats are okay). Finding hats among a crowd these days is sometimes not too easy, so enjoy the fun of scrounging around to find the hats. When the transmitter gets six hats they line them up in a row on the table. The transmitter has to memorize who is the owner of each hat, and know to whom each belongs.

The test for the mindreader is to find each owner and place the correct hat on its owner's head. This is a humorous test, and as the transmitter knows to whom each hat belongs, it plays extremely well.

Things can sometimes get mixed up in performing this test, as the transmitter can forget to whom each hat belongs. If they do, and direct you incorrectly – they'll have to admit they are the one who made the mistake. Just proves the mindreader is no fake.

The Reunited Couple

You stand blindfolded while the transmitter finds an affectionate couple (girl with her boyfriend) in the audience. They have them stand, and then they reseat them, separately, in different parts of the auditorium.

The transmitter knows where the couple has been reseated.

Returning to the stage, the transmitter grips your wrist, and things commence. Picking up the impulses from the transmitter, you first locate the girl and then her boyfriend. Have her stand and go along with you. Continuing to pick up the impulses from the transmitter, you locate her boyfriend. Then have them tag along as you locate the two seats in which they were sitting side by side.

You can do it via Contact Mindreading. Audiences love this kind of thing – "oo la la, all the world loves those in love".

The Murder Mystery

The Murder Mystery is a favorite Contact Mindreading demonstration. A detective style mystery provides exciting entertainment. This effective mindreading routine holds that kind of appeal.

While you are out of the room, accompanied by a committee who make sure you behave yourself, the spectators decide upon a victim, a murderer, a place where the crime was committed, and a weapon. You have explained that in a real murder mystery the victim's body is usually hidden, but that in this case it would be more difficult to find the victim in the middle of live people. Therefore, the victim remains with the others.

The murderer remains with the others for the same reason, and the weapon used to commit the crime is hidden.

The transmitter must be familiar with the locations of the people and things used in the imagined crime.

When you return to the stage, the transmitter grips your left wrist and, one by one, concentrates on each location. You turn into a veritable Sherlock Holmes in this test of mental skill as you find the victim, the murderer, the location where the crime took place, and the weapon used in the killing.

The same modus operandi is used in performing this sensational presentation of Contact Mindreading as in other demonstrations. The potential for designing dramatic scenes in mindreading demonstrations is remarkable.

The Pin Test

This is a classic feat of Contact Mindreading.

You are escorted out of the room under committee control. In your absence, a member of the audience takes a pin and inserts it in the wall – in a spot plainly visible to the audience about on the level of your shoulders. They then withdraw the pin, and hide it somewhere in the room.

You are recalled and blindfolded. The transmitter grips your wrist, and *concentrates* and *wills* – step by step – that you first find the pin, wherever it has been hidden. You move to the general location of where the pin was stuck in the wall. Then, circling your hand around in narrowing circles – until you feel the proper impulse – you push the pin home in the spot where it was formerly inserted.

The feat plays great, but is not too difficult being only a modification of 'finding the spot', which you have learned how to do in your private practice.

The Reformed Tableau

This is a full stage demonstration.

You are escorted out of the room under control. While gone, several spectators come on stage and form a simple tableau group – the position of each person in the tableau being memorized by the transmitter. The group disassembles and remains standing on stage.

You are recalled, and the transmitter *concentrates* and *wills* you to reconstruct the tableau.

You go, in turn, to each person who formed a part in the original tableau. Along with your transmitter, you look each deep in their eyes, as though reading their mind, and ask them to think of their position in the tableau. Of course, your real impression is coming from the transmitter gripping your wrist, but this action creates the impression that you are reading the person's mind directly. When you get the position impulse, reform the person, and tell them to stay in that position like a statue.

Person after person you handle like that, until you reform the entire tableau.

The feat plays as a full stage production, with lots of action and laughs as the people take odd positions and stand like statues forming the tableau.

The laughs continue as you reform the tableau. Take your time, and make a few mistakes once in a while in repositioning a person; then finally get it right. IT'S SHOWMANSHIP!

Practice this feat thoroughly in private with friends before you attempt it on stage.

Advice to the performer

In performing mindreading you are demonstrating a most marvelous phenomenon that requires great skill. You are a Concert Artist. Demand that respect from your audience.

Remember, you are the captain of your ship.

In presenting a Mindreading Show, less plays better than more. In other words, present some effective feats, but limit the number of feats you do. Mindreading is concentrated entertainment. A few feats, well presented, is all the show you need to become an ever to be remembered entertainer.

MINDREADING IS MIRACULOUS!

Chapter Nineteen

Mindreading Theater Drama

Chapter Nineteen

Mindreading Theater Drama

Using your imagination you can develop your mindreading demonstrations into full-stage productions. This developing of THE MURDER MYSTERY (described in the foregoing Chapter) shows the way.

For example, the effect can be presented in a Courtroom Set. The theme of the drama, as described to the audience, is that a murder has been committed. The victim (in this case) is still among the living, the police inspector has located a witness and the murder weapon has been found.

The cast is assembled on stage and twelve jurors are invited up. They take their seats in the jury box at side of stage. A dignified person is invited to play the role of judge. They come forward and take the judge's chair and are given the role of Master of Ceremonies for the drama. The crime must be solved by you, through MINDREADING.

A young man or woman is invited to play the role of the lawyer (the lawyer is also the transmitter in the drama and needs to be clear about the story). You, the mindreader are the detective who must solve the case, e.g. locate the person who plays the part of the victim, the person who plays the part of the murderer, the person who plays the part of the witness to the crime and the person who plays the part of the police inspector. You also must identify the location of the murder weapon (a toy pistol).

Identifying which person is which, and finally the location of the pistol, which will be hidden in the audience is quite a dramatic task – it all rests in the head of you, the MINDREADER.

You are taken out of the room, under surveillance of a Committee.

Four cards, of a size that is easily visible, are used as props in the drama. On one card is printed VICTIM; on one card is printed MURDERER; on one card is printed WITNESS; on one card is printed POLICE INSPECTOR. The final prop is the murder weapon – the toy pistol.

A member of the jury invites four people to come on stage to assume the different roles; each is given a card identifying their part – VICTIM, MURDERER, WITNESS, POLICE INSPECTOR. These people come on stage and each takes a chair.

Each places their identifying card, face down, on their lap.

All this while you, the mindreader, playing the role of detective, have been out of the room and you 139do not know which person is which. Your job is to decide, by mindreading, which is which, as they are seated before you. The audience and cast on stage are all on the IN. To add to your mindreading complications, the lawyer has hidden the murder weapon in the audience. As the detective you must also find the pistol amongst the big crowd.

You are invited back to the stage. The Committee testifies you have continually been under control. The drama mounts. Will you or will you not be able to tell who is who in the staged play?

The judge says, "Find the VICTIM".

Taking the lawyer's hand, you walk over to one of the four and pick up the face down card ...you show it displays VICTIM. Test correct.

The judge says, "Find the MURDERER".

Again you walk over to one in the row and pick up the card ... you show it displays MURDERER. Test correct.

The judge says, "Find the WITNESS".

You walk over to that person and hold up the card, WITNESS. Test correct.

There is no point in locating the police inspector as they are obviously the person who is left. So, the judge says, "Find the MURDER WEAPON".

Taking the lawyer along with you, you locate the pistol that has been hidden in the audience. The cast is dismissed amidst applause. You, the performer take a bow.

This illustrates how theatrical drama can be built around the Mindreading Demonstrations. Great show, but not hard to do. The further apart the chairs that the different people to be identified are seated in are spaced, the easier it is to perform.

In fact, once the impulse comes through and you know which chair the particular person is seated in you can even drop the hand of the transmitter and walk alone to the person and display the identifying card.

The field is wide open for a big time mindreading show, just as it is for a big time hypnotism show.

Combined together - WOW!

Chapter Twenty

Designing Your
Mindreading Show

Chapter Twenty

Designing Your Mindreading Show

In presenting a Mindreading Show, you are moving into unfamiliar territory so you must have an introduction that is explicit and tells the audience what the show is all about. This Chapter will give you some ideas you can use to create your own introduction, as you create your original show.

"Ladies and Gentlemen …

Welcome to a CONCERT OF MINDREADING. What you will witness may seem mysterious, as we venture into unexplored realms. Unexplored now, but very likely well known in the future.

All human communication is mindreading, which is mind to mind communication. Speech is verbalized mind communication between people, but it is so common in our daily experience that we no longer regard it as mysterious. Actually, speech is very mysterious and conjures great power. It has been said, 'The right word, spoken at the right time, in the right way, can change the world'.

I BELIEVE IT!

What you will witness may seem mysterious, as it takes us into the unfamiliar territory, which is mind to mind communication without speech. It is a silent mental communication. It has been called telepathy. What you will witness is absolutely genuine.

I present these experiments for you in our current space and time. In the future, it is not unlikely you will be doing such silent mental communication yourself. What I present for you now, you actually have the power to do yourself. As you take part in these demonstrations, you will instinctively know this is true.

Telepathy is really a form of mental radio. Like the telephone, at first it required a wire connection. Today much telephoning is wireless. Mindreading is much that way. It starts with a wired connection and advances to a wireless connection. I will show you what I mean.

In demonstrating mindreading to you, two people are involved. One is the TRANSMITTER and the other is the RECEIVER. In all of these experiments I will be the receiver, and the transmitter will be taken from a variety of volunteers from the audience who boldly adventure to explore the uncharted realm of mindreading. In these experiments we must establish a rapport between us, which is much like the contact of a handshake. A handshake commences a bond of friendship. Such friendship is the rapport that makes it possible to show you MINDREADING.

Let us begin ..."

An opening speech of such nature will get your show started. Where you go from there is up to you, as you create your own show. What you will present will be largely what you have learned how to do in this book. When you master mindreading there are many feats you can perform. Dip in deep and use what you like best.

We would not presume to tell you which routines to use and which not to use. All are effective and entertaining. You must create your own show, as only then will it be an original. Like an original Van Gogh painting has great value, so does your original show. Be an original.

Get busy now and learn how to perform REAL Mindreading ... create your own show – creative artist that you are.

Chapter Twenty One

Advice for an Effective Mindreading Show

Chapter Twenty One

Advice for an Effective Mindreading Show

The Mindreading Tests described are classics. With practice you can perform every one of them perfectly. Once you get the knack of following the impressions (impulses) that come into you, it will almost seem that you are being verbally told what to DO and where to GO. Contact Mindreading is amazing. In fact, you will even amaze yourself at how proficient you can become at the art. Each performance increases your ability.

Here is some general advice ...

Do not take yourself too seriously when you perform. Be good-natured and enjoy what you are doing. Make your audience appreciate your unusual talent. Even more important, make them like you as an entertainer. As many a successful performer has said, "It is not what you do but how you do it that is important".

Do not become impatient if you do not progress as rapidly as you might wish. Remember, you are practically developing a 'Sixth Sense'. You are learning how to do what very few people know how to do. In fact, to many what you do seems utterly impossible. You are advancing to the stature of a unique entertainer.

Here is a further word about your volunteer transmitters:

If the person does not do their work properly, and you feel they are not concentrating and using their WILL effectively, do not hesitate to replace them. No offence intended. As a performer it is important that your show be a success. Simply tell the poor transmitter that the required rapport between you is not sufficiently developed as yet. Better luck next time.

On with the show!

The transmitter in mindreading demonstrations must be earnest and sincere. They must appreciate what you are doing and want you to succeed. In mindreading two people work together in harmony.

The transmitter must be as good a thought transmitter as you are a thought receiver. And remember, the audience is there to witness the unusual. They want things to work.

As occasionally happens, if your transmitter does not seem to be concentrating properly, tell them sincerely, "Please try harder now and concentrate your *mind* and *will* earnestly. Fix your mind on the right spot. Make a determined effort that I respond correctly to your thoughts. Remember, the success of a Mindreading Experiment depends as much on you as it does on me".

Every success you have in mindreading is a triumph. You are demonstrating the remarkable capacities of the human mind. Every member of the audience knows they have a mind and instinctively KNOWS that with proper training they, too, could do the wonderful things you do.

That is why mindreading is such great entertainment!

You are demonstrating the future. You are demonstrating future human talent yet to come. You will thrill your audience.

It is breathtaking entertainment. Many times utter silence reigns. Quite frankly, Mindreading Entertainment is in a class by itself.

Chapter Twenty Two

Intimate Mindreading Experiments

Chapter Twenty Two

Intimate Mindreading Experiments

These intimate mindreading demonstrations are great for performing in close-up situations, at private parties, as informal entertainment etc. You can present them anywhere. They are great for getting publicity. Perform one or so of these in a newspaper office for the editor and you'll likely get a feature story.

Spotting the Card

Spread a deck of playing cards in a jumble, face up on the table. Mix the cards as much as you wish.

Have yourself taken out of the room under control. While you are absent, the spectators gather about the table and decide on one card in the jumble. You are then recalled.

Returning, you have the transmitter stand by your left side near the table on which the jumble of cards is spread. You grip their right hand in your left, which leaves your right hand free to pass over the cards.

The transmitter must know the location of the decided-upon card. That is, they must know where to spot it – just the location of the card in the jumbled group. What the card is is not important. *The transmitter concentrates on where the card is in the group, and wills you to spot it.*

You pick up a sharp pointed knife in your free hand, pass it over the cards several times, and then begin circling above the jumble of cards. Gradually make the circles smaller and smaller above the cards, until your hand becomes central, above one card. If correct, the impulse will come to plunge the knife into that card. Do so, and bring up the knife with the spotted card impaled on its blade. You have correctly spotted the card amidst the jumbled group by mindreading.

The Checker Move

Place a checkerboard on the table and assemble the red and black checkers on it, in game formation. While you are absent from the room, the spectators decide on one checker that they want to be picked up and replaced on the board in a selected position.

The transmitter must know which checker is to be picked up, and where it is to be replaced on the board.

You are recalled.

As in the foregoing test, grip the transmitter's right hand in your left, and move your free hand over the checkers on the checkerboard. Circle around above the checkers, while the transmitter mentally directs you. Make your circling smaller and smaller and smaller until your hand hovers over one particular checker. Pause.

Wait for the, "Correct. That's it!" impulse to come in from the transmitter. When you get it, reach down and pick up the checker upon which your hand has centered. You will be right on target.

Now, take the checker you have picked up in your right hand, and circle it above the checkerboard. Continue until the impression comes in from the transmitter, "That's it. Place it there". Place the checker on the board in that position. Again, you will be right on target.

Locating a Selected Card

While you are absent from the room under control, the assembled spectators shuffle a deck of cards and all together they decide on one card in the deck. You are recalled.

Take the cards and spread them out face-up on the table. Take the transmitter's right hand in your left, as usual. The transmitter knows the name of the selected card and must *will* you to find it.

Using your free right hand, pick up the cards from the table one at a time. As you pick up each card, slowly 'weigh' it in your hand, so to speak, and then place it aside if you receive no, "Stop" impulse from the transmitter.

Continue thus to pick up a card – one by one – and 'weigh' the card each time. When the selected card is picked up, somehow it will seem heavier, and you will *know* it is the card the spectators privately selected.

Exactly what this 'weighing feeling' is like is difficult to describe. You will have to learn to recognize it by experience. You will definitely sense a 'heaviness' in the card when it is the selected card.

Perform this feat slowly, shaking your head, "No" just before you discard a card.

If by the lack of concentration of the transmitter, you fail to sense the 'heavy feeling' when you pick up the right card, the shake of the head will be apt to arouse them to exert their *will* more actively, and you will feel the mental impulse come in as a sense of heaviness in the selected card.

This is a very effective mindreading feat; just take your time in performing it. Make several feints at each card you pick up – weighing it – and finally discarding it. Continue until you sense the 'heavy' card. You'll be right on target.

A Simplified Contact Method for Intimate Mindreading Experiments

Instead of gripping hands by your left side, have the transmitter rest their right hand on the back of your freely moving right hand … placing their right hand over yours, with the tips of their fingers resting on your fingers between your knuckles and first joints. Using this method of contact between transmitter and receiver often proves effective.

The Chosen Number Test

While you are conducted out of the room the spectators decide on a number from one to ten. Everyone is to think of the chosen number; especially the transmitter. The transmitter is to think of the *shape* of the selected number instead of just thinking of the number.

For instance, if the number 8 is thought of, the transmitter should think of the shape of the figure and not the word 'eight'. With this 'shape' mental handling the numbers come through most clearly.

If performed on stage, you can demonstrate the test using a whiteboard and heavy black marking pen. Draw large and make a good display. Hold the marking pen in your free hand, while the contact with the transmitter is maintained by having them rest their right hand on the back of your right hand.

The impulse to draw the shape of the number will come through nicely.

Alternatively, hold the marking pen in your free right hand over the whiteboard, while the contact with transmitter is with your left hand gripping the transmitter's right hand by your side.

Start by circling your hand around the surface of the whiteboard. Then bring your marking pen to a starting point, which you will soon perceive. Hold your fingers pressing lightly forward and impart to your hand a trembling, vibratory motion, as if hesitating about the next movement, saying at the same time to the transmitter, "*Will hard now* … Will the direction to me; the shape of the number".

Soon you will begin to get an impression of 'right' or 'left' or 'up' or 'down', and let your pen mark on the whiteboard what comes in. You will find yourself drawing the shape of the chosen number.

Drawing by Mindreading Test

Give a member of the audience a pen and paper and ask them to draw a figure of a person, or whatever they wish. You have no idea what picture they have drawn.

You are blindfolded.

You can use the person who drew the picture as your transmitter in this experiment, if you wish.

Stand in front of the whiteboard with a marking pen. Have the person who drew the picture stand by your side with their hand resting lightly on top of yours. Then have them hold their picture before their eyes, so they can concentrate on its shape. In their mind, they draw the picture line by line.

You, in turn, draw the picture line by line. Remember, the transmitter is always to transmit shape, not the name of the object drawn.

Practice this Drawing by Mindreading Test, so you can perform it well. It is an effective demonstration for the stage.

Chapter Twenty Three

Opening a Safe by Mindreading

Chapter Twenty Three

Opening a Safe by Mindreading

This is the *piece de resistance* of Intimate Mindreading Experiments. Perform the feat of opening the private safe in the office of a newspaper editor and probably you'll get a full-page story. Perform it in the executive office of a corporation and you'll very likely be booked for a corporate show.

The official office safe is usually regarded as the citadel for most valuable papers, and its combination is a private matter known to very few people in a company. So, when you are able to read the mind of a person who knows the safe's combination, your skill is instantly recognized.

Opening a safe by mindreading is an advanced experiment, but with practice you can do it, as it is based on the same subtle principles of Contact Mindreading that you have learned. Just as long as the person who grips your hand knows the combination that opens the safe and keeps careful watch as you turn the dial, you can do it.

How to open a safe by Contact Mindreading

Have the projector (transmitter) of the safe's combination grip your left hand, while you kneel down before the safe to spin the dial that opens the safe. When performed in proper sequence, the safe will open.

Start by slowly turning the dial, which has numbers along its rim, to the right. Instruct the projector to concentrate on which number the dial is to be stopped at in its first spin, and when the first number is reached to think STOP. Move the dial slowly so the numbers can be seen by the projector as they pass by. You will receive a definite impulse to *stop* at the correct first number for the first turn.

Most private safes open by three dial turnings: first to the right; then backward to the left; then again right to a third number. Once the first number is reached, pause, and then slowly turn the dial backwards to the left. When the correct number of this backward turn of the dial is reached, again you will receive the impulse to *stop*.

Then, another turn of the dial to the right is made, and you *stop* on the mental impulse to stop. You have mentally fathomed the combination. Just turn the handle and the safe will open.

You can open most any safe in any office by using this method, provided the editor or executive will concentrate on the combination correctly. The very importance of the feat will secure your anxious attention on the part of the projector, and you will receive strong 'clues' as you proceed.

For success in this remarkable demonstration of invading the privacy of this most private information (the safe's secret combination) is the correct interpretation of the impulses you receive. With your cultivation of the skill this can become a mastery demonstration.

Needless to say, keep the modus operandi to yourself. Expand it into a profound mystery, as you are mentally penetrating into the realm of most private information.

Opening a Padlock or Combination Lock by Mindreading

Here is another very effective Intimate Mindreading Experiment. Have a large padlock locked with its key, and then mix this lock-opening key among other keys of similar nature. They look very much the same and, unless you know which key is the one that opens the padlock, it is impossible to tell which is the correct key. Only the owner of the padlock knows.

In performing this demonstration, lock the padlock and mix the opening key among the dozen similar keys. Then spread the keys out in a row on the table.

Have the person who knows which key is the only one which will open the padlock grip your hand. Pass your free hand over the row of keys, picking each up in turn, while the projector concentrates on which is the correct key. When you pick up the padlock opening key you will get a definite impulse that it is the correct key (sometimes the impulse comes that the particular key seems heavier than the rest). Replace the key on the table among the others. THEN RESPOND TO

THE IMPULSE and again pick up that key. Insert it in the padlock and open the lock.

The effect is complete.

You can open a combination-type padlock in the same way you open a safe, e.g. a turn to the right, STOP. A turn backwards to the left, STOP. Another turn to the right until the impulse comes in to STOP.

The combination-type padlock will snap open.

Chapter Twenty Four

Mindreading Misdirection

Chapter Twenty Four

Mindreading Misdirection

Misdirection is a term well-known to magicians. It means directing the audience's attention in the wrong direction to increase the mystery of the effect. As entertainment you can use this principle effectively to increase mindreading mystery.

For example:

> In your INTRODUCTION to the show, you can state how the mind to mind communication of telepathy can be likened to transmitting thought along a wire as in a telephone. You have an excellent chance for misdirection here.
>
> Explain that you will show how thoughts can be transmitted over a wire connection, in the demonstration of mindreading you will perform.
>
> Display a foot length of stiff wire and have the transmitter firmly grip one end of the wire while you grip the other. Present all of your demonstrations using this 'wire connection' rather than by hand-on-body connection. It works just as well.

This is Mindreading Misdirection. Often it increases the wonderment. In such a method of performing it seems that since you have no direct bodily contact, the mental messages that come through must be, as you explained in your introduction, via mental telephone.

This style of working with a wire connection between you turns the Mindreading Show into even more of a current day marvel.

As you are aware, you can hold a foot length of stiff wire between yourself and the transmitter, and the direction impulses will come through to you over the wire. Sometimes it is even found that a wire-held connection between the transmitter and the receiver actually amplifies the reception of the impulses even more than in hand to hand connection.

Such misdirection of modus operandi adds to the apparent technology of THE MAGIC OF THE MIND.

Magic Wand Mindreading

Almost every magician has a magic wand. You can get one from my magic shop for a dollar or two.

A magic wand has traditional glamor. Magic wands are historic. Merlin had a magic wand. Even children know about magic wands – they read about them in fairytales. Every princess, prince, sorcerer or wizard has a magic wand.

Remember your show is for entertainment; it is not an academic dissertation. You have perfect licence to tell of the historic glamor of the magic wand. That's show business.

Introduce a magic wand and hold it on display as you tell your audience the story of its magical powers. Explain that by using a magic wand you can entertain them even more with mindreading enchantment.

And so …

You can use a magic wand throughout your entire show. Have the transmitter hold one end of the magic wand while you hold the other end. You hold the magic wand between you in all your demonstrations. And, if you wish, after each success in a Mindreading Test, you can give credit to the magic wand and have it take a bow. Yes, let it salute the audience, as you dip it forward.

In all the Mindreading Demonstrations you perform, you will find that holding the magic wand between you and the transmitter conveys and amplifies the impulses and impressions, just as does the stiff length of wire.

I like to use The Magic Wand – IT'S ENTERTAINMENT.

Chapter Twenty Five

Non-Contact Mindreading

Chapter Twenty Five

Non-Contact Mindreading

Telepathy is a phenomenon that happens continuously between people on a subjective level. Non-Contact Mindreading presents telepathy on an objective level.

Non-Contact Mindreading is demonstrating mindreading without a direct contact with the transmitter. It is telepathy.

The more experienced a person becomes with Contact Mindreading the more Non-Contact Mindreading will manifest itself. Until one gets exceedingly expert, Non-Contact Mindreading is not recommended for public performance, but for private entertainment it is fascinating. It advances into telepathic communication. The more a person can develop this ability, the greater mindreader they will become.

While Contact Mindreading is wonderful, Non-Contact Mindreading is even more wonderful, as is the comparison of the conventional wire telephone to current wireless telephone.

How? Why? What?

Some theories have been advanced. Popular is the Pineal Gland Theory.

The Pineal Gland Theory

The Pineal Gland Theory comes out of Yoga tradition. In India, telepathy is not regarded as theory but as fact.

The Pineal Gland is a small gland, cone-shaped, and of a reddish-gray color, situated in the brain, in about the middle of the skull, nearly above the top of the spinal column. It is a compact mass of nervous cellular tissue, containing a quantity of what has been called 'brain sand', which appears as very small particles of gritty matter.

Occidental anatomists confess they have no knowledge of the purpose and functions of the Pineal Gland. However, the Yogis state it is the ESP (Extra Sensory Perception) center of the brain forming a connection with the mind, which is directed by the self

(Consciousness). Its function is to receive thoughts directly in mind to mind communication. In other words, it is the center for transmitting and receiving telepathy within the brain. That is to say, it is the organic instrument for MINDREADING.

As a person advances in mastering Contact Mindreading, there will come times when they seem able to do away with the physical contact. In experimenting, there will come times when they will loosen their hold upon direct contact with the transmitter. Such an experience often comes as a personal surprise.

A telepathic non-contact experiment you can try with a friend is to have them hold a number of beads (of which they know the number). In the experiment, endeavor to *will* the receiver to 'guess' the right number. A similar experiment can be tried with cards. When the receiver endeavors to guess the color, suit, and denomination of the selected card.

Using the term 'guess' requires caution, for guessing is a conscious effort, and mindreading occurs through subconscious effort. In fact, psychic skills are always best accomplished by making the effort to perform them without effort. Adults often have difficulty in understanding this, as it is so common to feel that effort must be made in order to accomplish anything worthwhile. This is entirely contrary to Nature: a tree grows to be a tree without making effort to grow to be a tree. Nature is allowed to manifest itself. Developing the skill of Non-Contact Mindreading is just like that. Don't make effort to make it happen. Just afford it the opportunity to develop on its own.

As was observed in the first chapter of this book, the Creery children developed their skill at mindreading without making special effort to develop it. Children seem to have natural gifts for developing psychic talents, such as Non-Contact Mindreading, if they are left alone and aren't told they can't do what they can do. The Creery children became good mindreaders by making a game of it. A game is played to be enjoyed, not to be struggled with to play. That is the root meaning of 'make the effort without effort'. It is the way of great artists.

The Willing Game

The Creery children developed their mindreading skills by playing the Willing Game – just for the fun of it. If you wish to develop Non-Contact Mindreading talent, why not follow their example e.g. play the Willing Game with friends just for the fun of it.

In playing the Willing Game you stand in the center of the room, and the other people there, altogether *will* how you are to move: 'to the right'; then 'forward'; then' a little lower down', etc., etc. ... you can find an object for the group in this way. In playing the Willing Game there is no individual transmitter or contact with anyone. It is a group energy experience sending out telepathic commands. The more fun you make it, the better it plays.

Just as in Contact Mindreading, the group players concentrate on and *will* the central player to respond *one step at a time*, and should not be concerned with thoughts of succeeding steps. Just take your time in playing the Willing Game. ENJOY! playing the Willing Game – just for the fun of it. It is a great way to develop Non-Contact Mindreading talents. Play it often with harmonious friends.

Long Distance Telepathic Experiments

When you begin to get results in close-up experiments, then try some long distance telepathy. It seems that thoughts are of such a frequency they travel through hyperspace. That is to say, *just think a thought and it is there*. This has been commented on before.

Arrange to try some experiments with a friend in a distant place, just for the fun of it. Arrange for the experiment to be at a time both agree on. Then when ready to experiment together, the transmitter sits in their room alone, at the appointed time; they gaze at some simple object, say, a knife, a glass, a book, or whatever. This is to help concentrate the mind without distractions. This makes the mind grow quiet. A quiet mind is a mind that can concentrate on specific things ... in this case concentrating on whatever experiment has been arranged. Try it first by experimenting in transmitting the image of the object that has been gazed upon. The transmitter makes a clear mental picture of it, and then wills this picture to be reproduced in the distant person's (receiver's) mind. The receiver is relaxing in a receptive state, at the mutually agreed time arranged for the experiment. When you make a transmission of a certain object – as an experiment – with the distant person, do not think of its name; think of its shape.

The receiver on the distant end then draws the image of the object that comes into their mind. The success of distant mind to mind communication (telepathy) can then be checked. If you are interested, try such experiments together – sending thought to a distant friend with whom you enjoy a mutual interest. In other words, with whom you have rapport. Don't be concerned with the success or failure of the distant transmission experiment.[5] Make it a game you play together, just for the fun of playing the game.

Sometimes results can be surprising.

You are practicing Contact Mindreading. Why not also practice Non-Contact Mindreading? The two phases of mind communication dovetail together. Each augments the other.

Have fun and become a MASTER MINDREADER.

---

[5] *Distance does not necessarily mean "far distance". It simply means experiment with someone not in your immediate proximity. Mileage has no meaning to telepathy.*

Chapter Twenty Six

A Brief Review of Successful Mindreading

Chapter Twenty Six

A Brief Review of Successful Mindreading

As the mastering of Mindreading takes you into a completely new dimension of human communication, it is well to pause en route for a brief review of what you have learned thus far. Here are a dozen points, in the order of the text, associated with the performing of REAL Mindreading.

1. Mindreading is not a myth it is a fact. Yet, it is so unknown by the average person as to seem very much a mystery.

2. Mindreading is mind-to-mind communication without speech. It is silent communication, sometimes accomplished via a physical connection (such as a grip upon the wrist) and sometimes without.

3. Mindreading with a physical connection is known as Contact Mindreading. With no physical connection it is known as Telepathy.

4. Mindreading takes place between two people to accomplish experiments that to many lie within the realm of the unknown. Shall we say the realm of the magician?

5. In Mindreading demonstrations, the person who sends the thoughts – via concentration and willing on the reception of the thought by another is known as the TRANSMITTER. The transmitter's role in the mindreading experiment is active. In a Mindreading Show the transmitter is a volunteer who agrees to experiment with Mindreading.

6. In Mindreading demonstrations, the person who receives the thoughts, and responds to them, whatever they may be, is the performer who initiates the demonstrations. The performer is the gifted person who can read minds by receiving thoughts, and is known as the RECEIVER. The receiver's role is to present the show and be passively receptive to the transmitter's mental directions.

7. The performer (receiver) learns of visualization and body-awareness, which increase sensitivity to the input of thought ... important to successful mindreading demonstrations.

8. The performer (receiver) learns how to perform Contact Mindreading. The skill is developed by private practicing with friends. The importance of harmonizing (developing rapport) via Rhythmic Breathing is practiced along with the transmitter's instruction in how to project their thoughts ... the receiver learns how to experience and respond to incoming thoughts.

9. Thoughts from the transmitter are sent to the receiver by step-by-step directions of what the receiver is to do.

10. Thoughts from the transmitter are felt by the receiver in the form of impulses. The impressions are accurately directive. They are never guessed at.

11. The subjective phenomena of Hypnosis and the subjective phenomena of Mindreading can be used to subconsciously increase mindreading talent. Ref. Appendix: Self-Hypnosis for Mindreading.

12. The mastery of Mindreading comes by practice, practice, practice. Practice to open a whole new world of perception. It is an advancement of perception. Theatrical mindreading demonstrations are largely produced via assembled effective routines to entertain an audience who loves mystery and marvels at THE MAGIC OF THE MIND.

NOTE TO THE READER: As you become a master of REAL Mindreading, a whole new vista of the world will expand before you as your perception of ALL THAT IS advances.

I should pause a moment or two and comment on the forms of contact that can be made between the volunteer transmitter and the performer receiver. These can vary.

Some performers like to have the transmitter grip their left wrist. This leaves the right hand free to act as 'feeler'. Some performers have the transmitter touch the center of the receiver's forehead. Some performers have the transmitter rest their hand flat on the back of the receiver's hand.

A method I have found effective is to have the transmitter rest their flatly opened hand on crown of the receiver's head. The method used seems optional as long as contact is maintained. Use what you find works best for you, and is most convenient.

Chapter Twenty Seven

The Successful Stage Show

Chapter Twenty Seven

The Successful Stage Show

A successful stage show must have a smooth flow to its routine sequences (the way it is put together).

You can present an entire show of mindreading. You can present an entire show of hypnotism.

Or ...

If you wish, you can combine the two into a very effective presentation. Dunninger did this. Polgar did this. Kreskin does this. You can do this as you so elect, but the transition to each form of entertaining must be done smoothly.

Both Mindreading Demonstrations and Hypnotic Demonstrations carry their own mood. If you wish to combine the two forms of thought-provoking entertainment, you must artfully flow from one to the other. I saw an excellent example of the smooth flowing of mindreading to hypnotism performed by the Danish master, DeWaldoza.

DeWaldoza opened his show with Contact Mindreading by finding an object hidden in the audience while he was blindfolded. He then invited members of the audience to come on stage if they would like to learn how to do what he had done. Six people came on stage and were seated in a row. All were most anxious to learn. Equally the audience was interested.

DeWaldoza then truthfully explained how Contact Mindreading was accomplished. There was no exposure in this, as Contact Mindreading is a form of REAL Mindreading that takes real skill to accomplish.

DeWaldoza commenced by explaining to the group on stage and to the audience the principle of Ideomotor Action. He gave a pendulum (fishing weight tied to the end of a string) to each person on stage and showed them how to operate it, as explained in Chapter Fourteen of this book. All of the volunteers on stage soon had their little pendulums swinging merrily.

DeWaldoza selected a volunteer who had his pendulum swinging well, and had him stand. He explained that the body could be made to respond in the same way the pendulum did, by concentrating on the body swaying backwards. He then performed THE POSTURE SWAY EXPERIMENT[6] that causes the body to fall backwards in response to concentrating on the idea of falling backwards. He caught the person as they toppled over.

DeWaldoza performed the experiment with several others, explaining that the sensation of falling could be distinctly felt in response to the inner thought of falling backwards. He continued explaining that this inner sensation is what is felt in knowing where to go to find a hidden object, while having contact with the person who had hidden the object.

He asked for a volunteer who would like to try it. A person volunteered, and was blindfolded.

DeWaldoza borrowed an object (it was a comb) and hid it in the audience. He returned to the stage and took the blindfolded man down the steps to stand as he directed.

"I will take your wrist now and hold it gently, while I think where I have hidden the object. You do not know where it is, but I know. Thus, I will be the transmitter while you will be the receiver of my mental message. Just make yourself relaxed and passive, and go wherever you feel like going as the impulse comes into you. The sensation will be exactly as it was when you responded to the mental impulse to fall over backwards. I will hold your wrist but I will not lead you. You must lead me as you learn how to perform Contact Mindreading."

The man started to move and walked slowly down the aisle leading the performer. Step by step they went until the man stopped before a person seated on the aisle some twenty rows back from the front.

DeWaldoza then said, "Alright, now hold your free hand up and let it move in accordance to the impulses you feel coming into you – from my mind to your mind".

The man's hand went up and over, and searched inside the coat pocket of the spectator in front of whom he had stopped. He withdrew the comb. The audience was elated at the success of one of their own numbers performing the remarkable feat.

[6] *The New Encyclopedia of Stage Hypnotism*, p. 42.

Everyone, including the volunteer, was delighted.

Those on stage were dismissed and DeWaldoza went on to explain how the power of suggestion (the subconscious realization of an idea) accomplished the demonstration. He then went on to perform The Handlocking Test[7] in which the entire audience participated. Those to whom this proved successful were invited to come on stage and learn more about 'the magic of the mind'. The stage was filled to overflowing with volunteers.

This example of the smooth flowing of a demonstration of mindreading leading into demonstrations of hypnotism shows the artful handling of theater in the smooth flowing of the show.

As an entertainer, no matter what you do, always make your performance good theater.

[7] *The New Encyclopedia of Stage Hypnotism, p. 47.*

Appendix

Self-Hypnosis for Mindreading

Appendix

Self-Hypnosis for Mindreading

Self-Hypnosis For Mindreading is your private method for advancing your skills as a mindreader.

Hypnosis provides a rapid way to train your mind. A trained mind is a mind under control. A mind under the personal control of your consciousness is an advancement in perception. Advancement of perception is MINDREADING.

> *When mind is under control, the mind becomes like pure crystal reflecting equally, without distortion, the perception, the perceiver, and the perceived. It is through such mind that consciousness is known.*
>
> *Patanjali, 986 B.C.*
>
> *When mind is under control the mind becomes like pure crystal reflecting equally, without distortion, the perception, the perceiver, and the perceived. It is through such mind that REAL Mindreading is obtained.*
>
> *McGill, 2002 A.D.*

Combining the use of hypnosis to advance your perception in Contact Mindreading will have you presenting a Mindreading Show in record time. Non-Contact Mindreading will advance on its own. First, it is well to get some knowledge about hypnosis.

SELF-HYPNOSIS FOR MINDREADING is a breakthrough!

Some things about hypnosis

Self-Hypnosis provides a way to place your mind under your personal control, which is to make your mind think *when* you want it to think, to make your mind think *what* you want it to think, to make your mind *stop thinking* when you don't want it to think, and to become a *witness* to your thoughts.

When you thus become master of your mind, you become a MASTERMIND.

"We are what we think," is a classic quotation. What we think is based upon our perception of life. Great expertise in mindreading combines the skills of Contact Mindreading with Non-Contact Mindreading, which is 'direct perception'. That is the goal of the MASTER MINDREADER. The use of hypnosis can help you more quickly reach that goal. In this appendix, you will be shown an effective method you can use.

Mindreading is a subconscious activity of the mind. Hypnosis is a subconscious activity of the mind. Blending the two together, in a mutual process, you have here a method of self-hypnosis you can use to advance your skills as a mindreader plus save a lot of time in MASTERING MINDREADING.

Today, hypnosis is understood and used by more people than at any time in its history. Hypnotherapy has become a major profession. Check the Yellow Pages of telephone directories, and you will find dozens of hypnotherapists listed in every major city. Schools that teach hypnosis training abound. Hypnotism Stage Shows have become a popular form of entertainment. Hypnotism and mindreading produce a delightful concoction.

Hypnosis is produced by *the Power of Suggestion*. Hypnotic suggestions produce both the state and control. Hypnotic suggestions are defined as 'the subconscious realization of ideas'.

Mind is cited as having two main divisions: Conscious Mind and Subconscious Mind. They interact together. Conscious Mind is critical mind, and can be critical in affirming you can accomplish whatever it is you wish to accomplish. Subconscious Mind, once the proper affirmations are established, is never critical, but will help you achieve what it is that you wish to achieve.

In this book, you have learned how to perform REAL Mindreading objectively via practice. Combining it with Self-Hypnosis, you will learn how to perform REAL Mindreading *subjectively* as well.

The power of believing

Everything starts in pretending that it IS. With enough pretending soon one comes to believing that it IS. With enough believing soon one comes to making it reality. Imagination? I hope so, for imagination is the creative function of the mind. Everything that we know IS is the completed product of imagination.

The proper direction of imagination will turn you into a REAL Mindreader. There is no better way in the entire world to mentally create that reality.

Prelude to using Self-Hypnosis for developing mindreading talent

Study this book carefully and acquaint yourself with how to perform (and experience) all the various processes presented. In other words, learn them consciously. Practice them so fully you know how to perform them without thinking how to perform them. Thinking is a conscious phase of mind activity. While in hypnosis you become subjective and just do what you do (often automatically) without having to especially think about how to do it.

When you have thus become fully acquainted with each process used in the performance of mindreading, you are then ready to instill them in your subconscious phase of mind. That is to say, first you learn how to perform such as Contact Mindreading consciously, and, when ready, you then instill what you have learned into the subconscious. It then becomes instinctive to your nature, as the subconscious is the seat of instincts.

When you learn how to perform Contact Mindreading instinctively you become a MASTER.

Having so prepared yourself, you are ready to use SELF-HYPNOSIS FOR MINDREADING.

The Self-Hypnosis Method you will use

Get busy now and learn and use this method of conscious Self-Hypnosis. It will effectively advance your mindreading talents that will thrill your audiences.

Go into your private room alone, and darken the room. Place a candle on a table in front of a comfortable chair. If you have some meditative-type music handy, such as 'Golden Voyage', 'Ancient Echoes', etc. (obtainable at any Esoteric bookstore) start the music and play it softly – it makes a nice background for your self-hypnosis session.

Light the candle and take a seat in the comfortable chair. Relax back in the comfortable chair just like you would if you wanted to doze a little, and stare at the candle flame. Just stare and stare and stare for a little while. Let your mind grow calm, peaceful, and serene.

Allow whatever thoughts that come in to just pass through it. Just let your mind drift and drift. How quiet and calm you begin to feel, and your eyes are becoming tired staring at the candle. So blow out the candle and close your eyes as you rest back pleasantly in your comfortable chair. Your eyes are closed and it is dark, so you can drift, drift and drift.

Now, place the palm of a hand over each ear and press gently, and repeat *out loud* this suggestions formula:

> "I am becoming more and more relaxed in my comfortable chair. How quiet and peaceful my mind is becoming. How very sleepy I begin to feel. I am becoming more and more relaxed. I am becoming more and more sleepy – I am drifting down, down into the realm of hypnotic sleep where the suggestions I give myself become my reality. Down and down. I go … round and round I go, deeper and deeper into hypnosis. I am drowsy and sleepy, yet I am still a bit awake, and my conscious mind moves to one side, and my subconscious mind comes forth, ready and willing to accept these suggestions – which I give myself – and let them become my reality. Ready now. Subconscious mind accept these suggestions, and make them become my reality."

Now, let your hands drop down from your ears to your lap, and rest a few moments. Then, ready, set, go …

Replace your hands again flat over both ears and press in gently. Now, repeat the following affirmative suggestions about your developing skill in performing REAL Mindreading. Repeat them out loud to yourself so they RRRRRRRING through your head:

> "I believe in mindreading, and I know that I can do it. I can read a person's mind, as I am mentally directed to do this or that in mindreading demonstrations. It is easy for me to perform all the demonstrations. The impulses, which guide me where to go and what to do, come through to me distinctly. It is easy for me to do, with just a hand contact with the person. I can grip their hand or they can grip my wrist … or I can touch the center of their forehead to get their mental impressions that

come to me as impulses of where I am to go and what I am to do. Even more easily will the impulses come through to me when holding a length of wire or a magic wand between us. It is easy for me to do this, and my response is automatic and accurate every time ... with just a hand contact with the person who is the transmitter. The messages, impressions, impulses come through to me with clarity."

PAUSE AND REST FOR A WHILE

Let your hands drop from your ears into your lap, and doze a little, if you wish.

Don't rush the subconscious. There is no hurry. Just take your time, and allow your suggestions to sink into your subconscious phase of mind. You may doze, but your subconscious never sleeps, so while you rest it keep right on causing your desired suggestions to become reality (behavior) in your life. So rest and doze; even possibly sleep a little. Your subconscious will arouse you when it is ready to go on.

Replace your hands flat over your ears, and press in gently; then speak these suggestions out loud to yourself. Let them RRRRRRING through your head.

"I make instant rapport with each person I work with who is my volunteer transmitter in all demonstrations in mindreading I present.

I always give specific and correct instructions to each person who will be my transmitter, so they can perform their role correctly.

I perfectly receive telepathic impulse impressions that come through to me. I interpret them correctly ... quickly ... and to perfection. I perform each test perfectly.

I perform my Mindreading Demonstrations with showmanship. I am charming and charismatic when I perform. I love my audience. I have an intimate connection with my audience when I perform. I radiate love and goodwill to all who are before me."

PAUSE NOW.

Let your hands drop down from your ears into your lap. Just relax and go silent. Give your subconscious time to deeply absorb the suggestions you have given to develop your expertise as a performer. Always remember, it is not what you do but how you do it that is important.

Just wait, Wait, WAIT. Then replace your hands over your ears and speak out loud to yourself:

"My hypnosis session, for training my mind and body how to perform all the Mindreading Demonstrations I have learned, I perform to perfection. I receive and interpret the thought impulses that come through to me from the transmitter perfectly, to which I add my Non-Contact Mindreading Telepathic Insights, which makes me a Master Mindreader. My reactions are spontaneous, accurate and quick. Each day, in every way, I am becoming a better and better mindreader.

I AM AN ENTERTAINER.

My hypnosis session for training my mind and body for performing mindreading is now complete. I have advanced my skills. I will have my subconscious arouse me from hypnosis when my subconscious has affirmed that the performance of all of these hypnotic suggestions has become my reality. I will arouse myself from hypnosis feeling wonderful and fine. I am rapidly becoming a Master of REAL Mindreading.

I AM AN ENTERTAINER!"

Stop now and go silent, going deeper and deeper into hypnosis. You are becoming a master of your mind. Your subconscious mind will arouse you when the MASTERY OF MINDREADING suggestions have become *mentally set*. Drop into the realm of sleep and dreams a bit, if you elect. You will arouse elated!

And when you 'come back' you will sense deep inside yourself that you are becoming a Master Mindreader ... the proof is right before you as you present your Mindreading Demonstration better and better each time that you perform.

YOU ARE BECOMING A MINDREADING ENTERTAINER.

The effects of hypnosis, for accomplishing the goal of the achievement you have set for yourself are compounding. You can repeat your Self-Hypnosis for Mindreading session as often as you like. Each time you become a better mindreader in every way.

YOU WILL SOON BE READY TO PRESENT PUBLIC SHOWS.

Self-Hypnosis can be used not only for advancing your mindreading skill; it can be used to give you a better life in every way. Just plan your affirmative suggestions you wish to implant in your subconscious with thoughtful care.

Look upon your subconscious mind as your friend. It is at your service. Hypnosis brings it to attention, ready to aid you. Treat it as a personality, and address it with respect. Ask and it shall be given unto you.

When something is achieved, say, "THANK YOU!"

A Salute To The "Dean of American Hypnotists"

Manuscripts & Books By Ormond McGill

A Better Life Through Conscious Self-Hypnosis

Abundance Hypnosis

Advertising for the Independent Businessman

Art of Stage Hypnotism, The

Atomic Magic

Balancing Magic and Other Tricks

Battling AIDS with Your Mind

Dental Hypnosis

Dream Doctor Cases, The

Encyclopedia of Stage Illusions (Burling Hull – Coauthor)

Entertaining with Magic

Fooling the Public (Robert Bernhardt – Coauthor)

Fun of Collecting Cinderella Stamps and Labels

Grieve No More, Beloved – The Book of Delight

Hypnotism and Meditation

How to Plan Successful Suggestion-Formulas

How to Produce Miracles

Hypnotism and Mysticism Of India

Hypnotism and Yoga

Instantaneous Hypnosis Techniques

Into the Strange Unknown

Magic and Illusions of Lee Grabel, The

Magic with Soap Bubbles

Many Lives of Alan Lee, The (Irvin Mordes – Coauthor)

Mastering AIDS through Mastering Death

Mind Magic

Mysticism and Magic of India, The

New Encyclopedia of Stage Hypnotism, The

Paper Magic

Prelife Regression Therapy

Professional Office Hypnotherapy

Professional Stage Hypnotism

Psychic Magic

Religious Mysteries of the Orient

Science Magic: 101 Tricks You Can Do

Secret World of Witchcraft, The

Successful Suggestion Formulas for Hypnotherapy

3 New Hypnotherapy Techniques

21 Gems of Magic

Voice Magic

Way Out Is In, The (Charles Mignosa – Coauthor)

Wonderful Sex without Danger of AIDS

Books and manuscripts listed above are not all available at this time.

Some are in print; some are out of print; some are yet to be published.

The New Encyclopedia of Stage Hypnotism

Ormond McGill

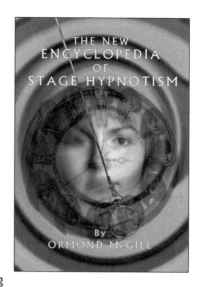

The most comprehensive text ever to be published on stage hypnotism, this book also has widespread therapeutic applications and contains work never previously published, providing new skills for even the most experienced practitioner of hypnosis. Ormond McGill totally demystifies stage hypnotism, dispels many of the myths associated with it, and leads us into his spellbinding world of hypnotic trance. A classic hypnosis text.

> *"Ormond McGill has produced a masterwork on Stage Hypnotism ... all inclusive of his previous work but with much new, up-to-date material added for today's mastery."*

Gil Boyne, President, American Council of Hypnotists Examiners

Hardback 640 pages 1899836020

www.crownhouse.co.uk

Grieve No More Beloved

The Book Of Delight

Ormond McGill

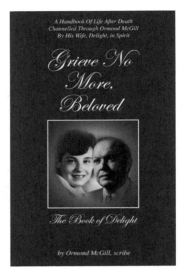

When Ormond McGill's beloved wife, Delight, died, he was grief-stricken. Yet even her untimely death could not break the bond of their love, and from 'beyond the veil' she began to contact her beloved husband, telling him of her life on the other side. Ormond wrote this book to bring solace to all those who hold in their hearts a loved one who has passed on, to bring them a message of hope and inspiration about the continuation of life. Here, with Ormond as her scribe, Delight answers many questions about life after death, bringing comfort and insight, joy and hope, and the proof that loved ones are never lost. A truly delightful book, and full of hope!

Hardback 126 pages 1899836004

Secrets of Dr. Zomb

The Autobiography of Ormond McGill

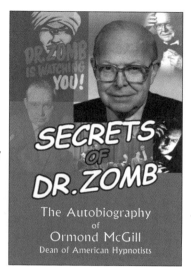

Have you ever dreamed of learning the deepest secrets of stage magic and hypnotism? This revelatory autobiography offers a fascinating insight into the life secrets of a magician and hypnotist of international reputation. Ormond McGill, the Dean of American Hypnotists, has hypnotized audiences all over the world with his exciting stage shows. Using original sketches, photographs and press material, Ormond explains techniques such as:

- Performing hypnosis on stage
- Acupressure hypnotic induction
- Self-hypnosis
- Mind control
- Real mindreading
- Past-life regression
- Yogi Pranayama practices

For everyone eager to learn more about the secrets of the stage show, this book provides wise counsel from the master performer. Join Ormond on his odyssey and share in a lifetime of rich and varied experiences. This is a performance not to be missed!

Hardback 500 pages (est) 189983687X

USA, Canada & Mexico orders to:
Crown House Publishing Company LLC
4 Berkeley Street, 1st Floor, Norwalk, CT 06850, USA
Tel: +1 203 852 9504, Fax: +1 203 852 9619
E-mail: info@CHPUS.com
www.CHPUS.com

UK, Europe & Rest of World orders to:
The Anglo American Book Company Ltd.
Crown Buildings, Bancyfelin, Carmarthen, Wales SA33 5ND
Tel: +44 (0)1267 211880/211886, Fax: +44 (0)1267 211882
E-mail: books@anglo-american.co.uk
www.anglo-american.co.uk

Australasia orders to:
Footprint Books Pty Ltd.
Unit 4/92A Mona Vale Road, Mona Vale NSW 2103, Australia
Tel: +61 (0) 2 9997 3973, Fax: +61 (0) 2 9997 3185
E-mail: info@footprint.com.au
www.footprint.com.au

Singapore orders to:
Publishers Marketing Services Pte Ltd.
10-C Jalan Ampas #07-01
Ho Seng Lee Flatted Warehouse, Singapore 329513
Tel: +65 6256 5166, Fax: +65 6253 0008
E-mail: info@pms.com.sg
www.pms.com.sg

Malaysia orders to:
Publishers Marketing Services Pte Ltd
Unit 509, Block E, Phileo Damansara 1, Jalan 16/11
46350 Petaling Jaya, Selangor, Malaysia
Tel : +03 7955 3588, Fax : +03 7955 3017
E-mail: pmsmal@streamyx.com
www.pms.com.sg

South Africa orders to:
Everybody's Books CC
PO Box 201321, Durban North, 4016, RSA
Tel: +27 (0) 31 569 2229, Fax: +27 (0) 31 569 2234
E-mail: warren@ebbooks.co.za